THE FOUR LOVES

Books by C. S. LEWIS

The Pilgrim's Regress
The Problem of Pain
The Screwtape Letters *and* Screwtape Proposes a Toast
Broadcast Talks
The Abolition of Man
Christian Behaviour
Beyond Personality
The Great Divorce
George MacDonald: An Anthology
Miracles
Transposition and Other Addresses
Mere Christianity
Surprised by Joy: The Shape of My Early Life
Reflections on the Psalms
The World's Last Night and Other Essays
The Four Loves
Letters to Malcolm: Chiefly on Prayer
Poems
Of Other Worlds: Essays and Stories
Letters of C. S. Lewis
Narrative Poems
A Mind Awake
On Stories: And Other Essays on Literature
Spirits in Bondage: A Cycle of Lyrics
The Business of Heaven: Daily Readings from C. S. Lewis
Present Concerns
All My Road Before Me: The Diary of C. S. Lewis, 1922–1927

For Children
THE CHRONICLES OF NARNIA:
The Lion, the Witch and the Wardrobe
Prince Caspian
The Voyage of the *Dawn Treader*
The Silver Chair
The Horse and His Boy
The Magician's Nephew
The Last Battle

Fiction
Out of the Silent Planet
Perelandra
That Hideous Strength
Till We Have Faces: A Myth Retold
The Dark Tower and Other Stories
Boxen: The Imaginary World of the Young C. S. Lewis

THE
FOUR LOVES

C. S. LEWIS

That our affections kill us not, nor dye.
—DONNE

A HARCOURT BRACE MODERN CLASSIC
HARCOURT BRACE & COMPANY

New York   San Diego   London

For information about permission to reproduce selections from this book,
please write to Permissions, Houghton Mifflin Harcourt Publishing Company,
215 Park Avenue South New York, NY 10003.

www.hmhbooks.com

Library of Congress Cataloging-in-Publication Data
Lewis, C. S. (Clive Staples), 1898–1963.
The four loves/C. S. Lewis
p.   cm.
Reprint. Originally published: New York: Harcourt, Brace, 1960.
ISBN 978-0-15-132916-8
1. Love—Religious aspects—Christianity.   I. Title
BV4639.L45   1991
241'.4—dc20   91-4033

Printed in the United States of America
DOC 25 24 23 22 21

To Chad Walsh

CONTENTS

THE FOUR LOVES

INTRODUCTION

"God is love," says St. John. When I first tried to write this book I thought that his maxim would provide me with a very plain highroad through the whole subject. I thought I should be able to say that human loves deserved to be called loves at all just in so far as they resembled that Love which is God. The first distinction I made was therefore between what I called Gift-love and Need-love. The typical example of Gift-love would be that love which moves a man to work and plan and save for the future well-being of his family which he will die without sharing or seeing; of the second, that which sends a lonely or frightened child to its mother's arms.

There was no doubt which was more like Love Himself. Divine Love is Gift-love. The Father gives all He is and has to the Son. The Son gives Himself back to the Father, and gives Himself to the world, and for the world to the Father, and thus gives the world (in Himself) back to the Father too.

And what, on the other hand, can be less like anything we believe of God's life than Need-love? He lacks nothing, but our Need-love, as Plato saw, is "the son of Poverty." It is the accurate reflection in consciousness of our actual nature. We are born helpless. As soon as we are fully conscious we discover loneliness. We need others physically, emotionally, intellectually; we need them if we are to know anything, even ourselves.

I was looking forward to writing some fairly easy panegyrics on the first sort of love and disparagements of the second. And much of what I was going to say still seems to me to be true. I still think that if all we mean by our love is a craving to be loved, we are in a very deplorable state. But I would not now say (with my master, MacDonald) that if we mean only this craving we are mistaking for love something that is not love at all. I cannot now deny the name *love* to Need-love. Every time I have tried to think the thing out along those lines I have ended in puzzles and contradictions. The reality is more complicated than I supposed.

First of all, we do violence to most languages, including our own, if we do not call Need-love "love." Of course language is not an infallible guide, but it contains, with all its defects, a good deal of stored insight and experience. If you begin by flouting it, it has a way of avenging itself later on. We had better not follow Humpty Dumpty in making words mean whatever we please.

Secondly, we must be cautious about calling Need-love "mere selfishness." *Mere* is always a dangerous word. No doubt Need-love, like all our impulses, can be selfishly indulged. A tyrannous and gluttonous demand for affection can be a horrible thing. But in ordinary life no one calls a child selfish because it turns for comfort to its mother; nor an adult who turns to his fellow "for company." Those, whether children or adults, who do so least are not usually the most selfless. Where Need-love is felt there may be reasons for denying or totally mortifying it; but not to feel it is in general the mark of the cold egoist. Since we do in reality need one another ("it is not good for man to be alone"), then the failure of this need to appear as Need-love in consciousness—in other words, the illusory feeling that it *is* good for us to be alone—is a bad spiritual symptom; just as lack of appetite is a bad medical symptom because men do really need food.

But thirdly, we come to something far more important. Every Christian would agree that a man's spiritual health is exactly proportional to his love for God. But man's love for God, from the very nature of the case, must always be very largely, and must often be entirely, a Need-love. This is obvious when we implore forgiveness for our sins or support in our tribulations. But in the long run it is perhaps even more apparent in our growing—for it ought to be growing—awareness that our whole being by its very nature is one vast need; incomplete, preparatory, empty yet cluttered, crying out for Him who can untie things that are now knotted together and tie up things that are still dangling loose. I do not say that man can never bring to God anything at all but sheer Need-love. Exalted souls may tell us of a reach beyond that. But they would also, I think, be the first to tell us that those heights would cease to be true Graces, would become Neo-Platonic or finally diabolical illusions, the moment a man dared to think that he could live on them and henceforth drop out the element of need. "The highest," says the *Imitation*, "does not stand without the lowest." It would be a bold and silly creature that came before its Creator with the boast "I'm no beggar. I love you disinterestedly." Those who come nearest to a Gift-love for God will next moment, even at the very same moment, be beating their breasts with the publican and laying their indigence before the only real Giver. And God will have it so. He addresses our Need-love: "Come unto me all ye that travail and are heavy-laden," or, in the Old Testament, "Open your mouth wide and I will fill it."

Thus one Need-love, the greatest of all, either coincides with or at least makes a main ingredient in man's highest, healthiest, and most realistic spiritual condition. A very strange corollary follows. Man approaches God most nearly when he is in one sense least like God. For what can be more unlike than fullness and need, sovereignty and humility, righteousness and penitence, limitless power and a cry for help? This paradox staggered me when I first ran into it; it also wrecked all my previous attempts to write about love. When we face it, something like this seems to result.

We must distinguish two things which might both possibly be called "nearness to God." One is likeness to God. God has impressed some sort of likeness to Himself, I suppose, in all that He has made. Space and time, in their own fashion, mirror His greatness; all life, His fecundity; animal life, His activity. Man has a more important likeness than these by being rational. Angels, we believe, have likenesses which Man lacks: immortality and intuitive knowledge. In that way all men, whether good or bad, all angels including those that fell, are more like God than the animals are. Their natures are in this sense "nearer" to the Divine Nature. But, secondly, there is what we may call nearness of approach. If this is what we mean, the states in which a man is "nearest" to God are those in which he is most surely and swiftly approaching his final union with God, vision of God and enjoyment of God. And as soon as we distinguish nearness-by-likeness and nearness-of-approach, we see that they do not necessarily coincide. They may or may not.

Perhaps an analogy may help. Let us suppose that we are doing a mountain walk to the village which is our home. At mid-day we come to the top of a cliff where we are, in space, very near it because it is just below us. We could drop a stone into it. But as we are no cragsmen we can't get down. We must go a long way round; five miles, maybe. At many points during that *détour* we shall, statically, be farther from the village than we were when we sat above the cliff. But only statically. In terms of progress we shall be far "nearer" our baths and teas.

Since God is blessed, omnipotent, sovereign and creative, there is obviously a sense in which happiness, strength, freedom and fertility (whether of mind or body), wherever they appear in human life, constitute likenesses, and in that way proximities, to God. But no one supposes that the possession of these gifts has any necessary connection with our sanctification. No kind of riches is a passport to the Kingdom of Heaven.

At the cliff's top we are near the village, but however long we sit there we shall never be any nearer to our bath and our tea. So here; the likeness, and in that sense nearness, to Himself which God has conferred upon certain creatures and certain states of those creatures is something finished, built in. What is near Him by likeness is never, by that fact alone, going to be any nearer. But nearness of approach is, by definition, increasing nearness. And whereas the likeness is given to us—and can be received with or without thanks, can be used or abused—the approach, however initiated and supported by Grace, is something we must do. Creatures are made in their varying ways images of God without their own collaboration or even consent. It is not so that they become sons of God. And the likeness they receive by sonship is not that of images or portraits. It is in one way more than likeness, for it is union or unity with God in will; but this is consistent with all the differences we have been considering. Hence, as a better writer has said, our imitation of God in this life—that is, our willed imitation as distinct from any of the likenesses which He has impressed upon our natures or states—must be an imitation of God incarnate: our model is the Jesus, not only of Calvary, but of the workshop, the roads, the crowds, the clamorous demands and surly oppositions, the lack of all peace and privacy, the interruptions. For this, so strangely unlike anything we can attribute to the Divine life in itself, is apparently not only like, but is, the Divine life operating under human conditions.

I must now explain why I have found this distinction necessary to any treatment of our loves. St. John's saying that God is love has long been balanced in my mind against the remark of a modern author (M. Denis de Rougemont) that "love ceases to be a demon only when he ceases to be a god"; which of course can be re-stated in the form "begins to be a demon the moment he begins to be a god." This balance seems to me an indispensable safeguard. If we ignore it the truth that God is love may slyly come to mean for us the converse, that love is God.

I suppose that everyone who has thought about the matter will see what M. de Rougemont meant. Every human love, at its height, has a tendency to claim for itself a divine authority. Its voice tends to sound as if it were the will of God Himself. It tells us not to count the cost, it demands of us a total commitment, it attempts to over-ride all other claims and insinuates that any action which is sincerely done "for love's sake" is thereby lawful and even meritorious. That erotic love and love of one's country may thus attempt to "become gods" is generally recognised. But family affection may do the same. So, in a different way, may friendship. I shall not here elaborate the point, for it will meet us again and again in later chapters.

Now it must be noticed that the natural loves make this blasphemous claim not when they are in their worst, but when they are in their best, natural condition; when they are what our grandfathers called "pure" or "noble." This is especially obvious in the erotic sphere. A faithful and genuinely self-sacrificing passion will speak to us with what seems the voice of God. Merely animal or frivolous lust will not. It will corrupt its addict in a dozen ways, but not in that way; a man may act upon such feelings but he cannot revere them any more than a man who scratches reveres the itch. A silly woman's temporary indulgence, which is really self-indulgence, to a spoiled child—her living doll while the fit lasts—is much less likely to "become a god" than the deep, narrow devotion of a woman who (quite really) "lives for her son." And I am inclined to think that the sort of love for a man's country which is worked up by beer and brass bands will not lead him to do much harm (or much good) for her sake. It will probably be fully discharged by ordering another drink and joining in the chorus.

And this of course is what we ought to expect. Our loves do not make their claim to divinity until the claim becomes plausible. It does not become plausible until there is in them a real resemblance to God, to Love Himself. Let us here make no mistake. Our Gift-loves are really God-like; and among our Gift-loves those are most God-like which are most boundless and unwearied in giving. All the things the poets say about them are true. Their joy, their energy, their patience, their readiness to forgive, their desire for the good of the beloved—all this is a real and all but adorable image of the Divine life. In its presence we are right to thank God "who has given such power to men." We may say, quite truly and in an intelligible sense, that those who love greatly are "near" to God. But of course it is "nearness by likeness." It will not of itself produce "nearness of approach." The likeness has been given us. It has no necessary connection with that slow and painful approach which must be our own (though by no means our unaided) task. Meanwhile, however, the likeness is a splendour. That is why we may mistake Like for Same. We may give our human loves the unconditional allegiance which we owe only to God. Then they become gods: then they become demons. Then they will destroy us, and also destroy themselves. For natural loves that are allowed to become gods do not remain loves. They are still called so, but can become in fact complicated forms of hatred.

Our Need-loves may be greedy and exacting but they

do not set up to be gods. They are not near enough (by likeness) to God to attempt that.

It follows from what has been said that we must join neither the idolaters nor the "debunkers" of human love. Idolatry both of erotic love and of "the domestic affections" was the great error of nineteenth-century literature. Browning, Kingsley, and Patmore sometimes talk as if they thought that falling in love was the same thing as sanctification; the novelists habitually oppose to "the World" not the Kingdom of Heaven but the home. We live in the reaction against this. The debunkers stigmatise as slush and sentimentality a very great deal of what their fathers said in praise of love. They are always pulling up and exposing the grubby roots of our natural loves. But I take it we must listen neither "to the over-wise nor to the over-foolish giant." The highest does not stand without the lowest. A plant must have roots below as well as sunlight above and roots must be grubby. Much of the grubbiness is clean dirt if only you will leave it in the garden and not keep on sprinkling it over the library table. The human loves can be glorious images of Divine love. No less than that: but also no more—proximities of likeness which in one instance may help, and in another may hinder, proximity of approach. Sometimes perhaps they have not very much to do with it either way.

LIKINGS AND LOVES
FOR THE SUB-HUMAN

Most of my generation were reproved as children for saying that we "loved" strawberries, and some people take a pride in the fact that English has the two verbs *love* and *like* while French has to get on with *aimer* for both. But French has a good many other languages on its side. Indeed it very often has actual English usage on its side too. Nearly all speakers, however pedantic or however pious, talk every day about "loving" a food, a game, or a pursuit. And in fact there is a continuity between our elementary likings for things and our loves for people. Since "the highest does not stand without the lowest" we had better begin at the bottom, with mere likings; and since to "like" anything means to take some sort of pleasure in it, we must begin with pleasure.

Now it is a very old discovery that pleasures can be divided into two classes; those which would not be pleasures at all unless they were preceded by desire, and those which are pleasures in their own right and need no such preparation. An example of the first would be a drink of water. This is a pleasure if you are thirsty and a great one if you are very thirsty. But probably no one in the world, except in obedience to thirst or to a doctor's orders, ever poured himself out a glass of water and drank it just for the fun of the thing. An example of the other class would be the unsought and unexpected pleasures of smell—the breath from a bean-field or a row of sweet-peas meeting you on your morning walk. You were in want of nothing, completely contented, before it; the pleasure, which may be very great, is an unsolicited, super-added gift. I am taking very simple instances for clarity's sake, and of course there are many complications. If you are given coffee or beer where you expected (and would have been satisfied with) water, then of course you get a pleasure of the first kind (allaying of thirst) and one of the second (a nice taste) at the same time. Again, an addiction may turn what was once a pleasure of the second kind into one of the first. For the temperate man an occasional glass of wine is a treat—like the smell of the bean-field. But to the alcoholic, whose palate and digestion have long since been destroyed, no liquor gives any pleasure except that of relief from an unbearable craving. So far as he can still discern tastes at all, he rather dislikes it; but it is better than the misery of remaining sober. Yet through all their permutations and combinations the distinction between the two classes remains tolerably clear. We may call them Need-pleasures and Pleasures of Appreciation.

The resemblance between these Need-pleasures and the "Need-loves" in my first chapter will occur to everyone. But there, you remember, I confessed that I had

had to resist a tendency to disparage the Need-loves or even to say they were not loves at all. Here, for most people, there may be an opposite inclination. It would be very easy to spread ourselves in laudation of the Need-pleasures and to frown upon those that are Appreciative: the one so natural (a word to conjure with), so necessary, so shielded from excess by its very naturalness, the other unnecessary and opening the door to every kind of luxury and vice. If we were short of matter on this theme we could turn on the tap by opening the works of the Stoics and it would run till we had a bathful. But throughout this inquiry we must be careful never to adopt prematurely a moral or evaluating attitude. The human mind is generally far more eager to praise and dispraise than to describe and define. It wants to make every distinction a distinction of value; hence those fatal critics who can never point out the differing quality of two poets without putting them in an order of preference as if they were candidates for a prize. We must do nothing of the sort about the pleasures. The reality is too complicated. We are already warned of this by the fact that Need-pleasure is the state in which Appreciative pleasures end up when they go bad (by addiction).

For us at any rate the importance of the two sorts of pleasure lies in the extent to which they foreshadow characteristics in our "loves" (properly so called).

The thirsty man who has just drunk off a tumbler of water may say, "By Jove, I *wanted* that." So may the alcoholic who has just had his "nip." The man who passes the sweet-peas in his morning walk is more likely to say, "How lovely the smell *is.*" The connoisseur after his first sip of the famous claret, may similarly say, "This *is* a great wine." When Need-pleasures are in question we tend to make statements about ourselves in the past tense; when Appreciative pleasures are in question we tend to make statements about the object in the present tense. It is easy to see why.

Shakespeare has described the satisfaction of a tyrannous lust as something

> *Past reason hunted and, no sooner had,*
> *Past reason hated.*

But the most innocent and necessary of Need-pleasures have about them something of the same character—only something, of course. They are not hated once we have had them, but they certainly "die on us" with extraordinary abruptness, and completely. The scullery tap and the tumbler are very attractive indeed when we come in parched from mowing the grass; six seconds later they are emptied of all interest. The smell of frying food is very different before and after breakfast. And, if you will forgive me for citing the most extreme instance of all, have there not for most of us been moments (in a strange town) when the sight of the word GENTLEMEN over a door has roused a joy almost worthy of celebration in verse?

Pleasures of Appreciation are very different. They make us feel that something has not merely gratified our senses in fact but claimed our appreciation by right. The connoisseur does not merely enjoy his claret as he might enjoy warming his feet when they were cold. He feels that here is a wine that deserves his full attention; that justifies all the tradition and skill that have gone to its making and all the years of training that have made his own palate fit to judge it. There is even a glimmering of unselfishness in his attitude. He wants the wine to be preserved and kept in good condition, not entirely for his own sake. Even if he were on his death-bed and was never going to drink wine again, he would be horrified at the thought of this vintage being spilled or spoiled or even drunk by clods (like myself) who can't tell a good claret from a bad. And so with the man who passes the sweet-peas. He does not simply enjoy, he feels that this fragrance somehow deserves to be enjoyed. He would blame himself if he went past inattentive and unde-lighted. It would be blockish, insensitive. It would be a shame that so fine a thing should have been wasted on him. He will remember the delicious moment years hence. He will be sorry when he hears that the garden past which his walk led him that day has now been swallowed up by cinemas, garages, and the new by-pass.

Scientifically both sorts of pleasure are, no doubt, relative to our organisms. But the Need-pleasures loudly proclaim their relativity not only to the human frame but to its momentary condition, and outside that relation have no meaning or interest for us at all. The objects which afford pleasures of appreciation give us the feel-ing—whether irrational or not—that we somehow owe it to them to savour, to attend to and praise them. "It would be a sin to set a wine like that before Lewis," says the expert in claret. "How can you walk past this garden taking no notice of the smell?" we ask. But we should never feel this about a Need-pleasure: never blame ourselves or others for not having been thirsty and therefore walking past a well without taking a drink of water.

How the Need-pleasures foreshadow our Need-loves is obvious enough. In the latter the beloved is seen in relation to our own needs, just as the scullery tap is seen by the thirsty man or the glass of gin by the alcoholic. And the Need-love, like the Need-pleasure, will not last longer than the need. This does not, fortunately, mean that all affections which begin in Need-love are transitory. The need itself may be permanent or recurrent. Another kind of love may be grafted on the Need-love. Moral principles (conjugal fidelity, filial piety, gratitude, and the like) may preserve the relationship for a lifetime. But where Need-love is left unaided we can hardly expect it not to "die on us" once the need is no more. That is why the world rings with the complaints of mothers whose grown-up children neglect them and of forsaken mistresses whose lovers' love was pure need—which they have satisfied. Our Need-love for God is in a different position because our need of Him can never end either in this world or in any other. But our awareness of it can, and then the Need-love dies too. "The Devil was sick, the Devil a monk would be." There seems no reason for describing as hypocritical the short-lived piety of those whose religion fades away once they have emerged from "danger, necessity, or tribulation." Why should they not have been sincere? They were desperate and they howled for help. Who wouldn't?

What Appreciative pleasure foreshadows is not so quickly described.

First of all, it is the starting point for our whole experience of beauty. It is impossible to draw a line below which such pleasures are "sensual" and above which they are "aesthetic." The experiences of the expert in claret already contain elements of concentration, judgment, and disciplined perceptiveness, which are not sensual; those of the musician still contain elements which are.

There is no frontier—there is seamless continuity—between the sensuous pleasure of garden smells and an enjoyment of the countryside (or "beauty") as a whole, or even our enjoyment of the painters and poets who treat it.

And, as we have seen, there is in these pleasures from the very beginning a shadow or dawn of, or an invitation to, disinterestedness. Of course in one way we can be disinterested or unselfish, and far more heroically so, about the Need-pleasures: it is a cup of water that the wounded Sidney sacrifices to the dying soldier. But that is not the sort of disinterestedness I now mean. Sidney loves his neighbour. But in the Appreciative pleasures, even at their lowest, and more and more as they grow up into the full appreciation of all beauty, we get something that we can hardly help calling *love* and hardly help calling *disinterested*, towards the object itself. It is the feeling which would make a man unwilling to deface a great picture even if he were the last man left alive and himself about to die; which makes us glad of unspoiled forests that we shall never see; which makes us anxious that the garden or bean-field should continue to exist. We do not merely like the things; we pronounce them, in a momentarily God-like sense, "very good."

And now our principle of starting at the lowest—without which "the highest does not stand"—begins to pay a dividend. It has revealed to me a deficiency in our previous classification of the loves into those of Need and those of Gift. There is a third element in love, no less important than these, which is foreshadowed by our Appreciative pleasures. This judgment that the object is very good, this attention (almost homage) offered to it as a kind of debt, this wish that it should be and should continue being what it is even if we were never to enjoy it, can go out not only to things but to persons. When it is offered to a woman we call it admiration; when to a man, hero-worship; when to God, worship simply.

Need-love cries to God from our poverty; Gift-love longs to serve, or even to suffer for, God; Appreciative love says: "We give thanks to thee for thy great glory." Need-love says of a woman "I cannot live without her"; Gift-love longs to give her happiness, comfort, protection—if possible, wealth; Appreciative love gazes and holds its breath and is silent, rejoices that such a wonder should exist even if not for him, will not be wholly dejected by losing her, would rather have it so than never to have seen her at all.

We murder to dissect. In actual life, thank God, the three elements of love mix and succeed one another, moment by moment. Perhaps none of them except Need-love ever exists alone, in "chemical" purity, for more than a few seconds. And perhaps that is because nothing about us except our neediness is, in this life, permanent.

Two forms of love for what is not personal demand special treatment.

For some people, perhaps especially for Englishmen and Russians, what we call "the love of nature" is a permanent and serious sentiment. I mean here that love of nature which cannot be adequately classified simply as an instance of our love for beauty. Of course many natural objects—trees, flowers and animals—are beautiful. But the nature-lovers whom I have in mind are not very much concerned with individual beautiful objects of that sort. The man who is distracts them. An enthusiastic botanist is for them a dreadful companion on a ramble. He is always stopping to draw their attention to particulars. Nor are they looking for "views" or landscapes. Wordsworth, their spokesman, strongly deprecates this. It leads to "a comparison of scene with scene," makes you "pamper" yourself with "meagre novelties of colour and proportion." While you are busying yourself with this critical and discriminating activity you lose what really matters—the "moods of time and season," the "spirit" of the place. And of course Wordsworth is right. That is why, if you love nature in his fashion, a landscape painter is (out of doors) an even worse companion than a botanist.

It is the "moods" or the "spirit" that matter. Nature-lovers want to receive as fully as possible whatever nature, at each particular time and place, is, so to speak, saying. The obvious richness, grace, and harmony of some scenes are no more precious to them than the grimness, bleakness, terror, monotony, or "visionary dreariness" of others. The featureless itself gets from them a willing response. It is one more word uttered by nature. They lay themselves bare to the sheer quality of every countryside, every hour of the day. They want to absorb it into themselves, to be coloured through and through by it.

This experience, like so many others, after being lauded to the skies in the nineteenth century, has been debunked by the moderns. And one must certainly concede to the debunkers that Wordsworth, not when he was communicating it as a poet, but when he was merely talking about it as a philosopher (or philosophaster), said some very silly things. It is silly, unless you have found any evidence, to believe that flowers enjoy the air they breathe, and sillier not to add that, if this were true, flowers would undoubtedly have pains as well as pleasures. Nor have many people been taught moral philosophy by an "impulse from a vernal wood."

If they were, it would not necessarily be the sort of moral philosophy Wordsworth would have approved. It might be that of ruthless competition. For some moderns I think it is. They love nature in so far as, for them, she calls to "the dark gods in the blood"; not although, but because, sex and hunger and sheer power there operate without pity or shame.

If you take nature as a teacher she will teach you exactly the lessons you had already decided to learn; this is only another way of saying that nature does not teach. The tendency to take her as a teacher is obviously very easily grafted on to the experience we call "love of nature." But it is only a graft. While we are actually subjected to them, the "moods" and "spirits" of nature point no morals. Overwhelming gaiety, insupportable grandeur, sombre desolation are flung at you. Make what you can of them, if you must make at all. The only imperative that nature utters is, "Look. Listen. Attend."

The fact that this imperative is so often misinterpreted and sets people making theologies and pantheologies and antitheologies—all of which can be debunked—does not really touch the central experience itself. What nature-lovers—whether they are Wordsworthians or people with "dark gods in their blood"—get from nature is an iconography, a language of images. I do not mean simply visual images; it is the "moods" or "spirits" themselves—the powerful expositions of terror, gloom, jocundity, cruelty, lust, innocence, purity—that are the images. In them each man can clothe his own belief. We must learn our theology or philosophy elsewhere (not surprisingly, we often learn them from theologians and philosophers).

But when I speak of "clothing" our belief in such images I do not mean anything like using nature for similes or metaphors in the manner of the poets. Indeed I might have said "filling" or "incarnating" rather than clothing. Many people—I am one myself—would never, but for what nature does to us, have had any content to put into the words we must use in confessing our faith. Nature never taught me that there exists a God of glory and of infinite majesty. I had to learn that in other ways. But nature gave the word *glory* a meaning for me. I still do not know where else I could have found one. I do not see how the "fear" of God could have ever meant to me anything but the lowest prudential efforts to be safe, if I had never seen certain ominous ravines and unapproachable crags. And if nature had never awakened certain longings in me, huge areas of what I can now mean by the "love" of God would never, so far as I can see, have existed.

Of course the fact that a Christian can so use nature is not even the beginning of a proof that Christianity is true. Those suffering from Dark Gods can equally use her (I suppose) for their creed. That is precisely the point. Nature does not teach. A true philosophy may sometimes validate an experience of nature; an experience of nature cannot validate a philosophy. Nature will not verify any theological or metaphysical proposition (or not in the manner we are now considering); she will help to show what it means.

And not, on the Christian premises, by accident. The created glory may be expected to give us hints of the uncreated; for the one is derived from the other and in some fashion reflects it.

In some fashion. But not perhaps in so direct and simple a fashion as we at first might suppose. For of course all the facts stressed by nature-lovers of the other school are facts too; there are worms in the belly as well as primroses in the wood. Try to reconcile them, or to show that they don't really need reconciliation, and you are turning from direct experience of nature—our present subject—to metaphysics or theodicy or something of that sort. That may be a sensible thing to do; but I think it should be kept distinct from the love of nature. While we are on that level, while we are still claiming to speak of what nature has directly "said" to us, we must stick to it. We have seen an image of glory. We must not try to find a direct path through it and beyond it to an increasing knowledge of God. The path peters out almost at once. Terrors and mysteries, the whole depth of God's counsels and the whole tangle of the history of the universe, choke it. We can't get through; not that way. We must make a *détour*—leave the hills and woods and go back to our studies, to church, to our Bibles, to our knees. Otherwise the love of nature is beginning to turn into a nature religion. And then, even if it does not lead us to the Dark Gods, it will lead us to a great deal of nonsense.

But we need not surrender the love of nature—chastened and limited as I have suggested—to the debunkers. Nature cannot satisfy the desires she arouses nor answer theological questions nor sanctify us. Our real journey to God involves constantly turning our backs on her; passing from the dawn-lit fields into some poky little church, or (it might be) going to work in an East End parish. But the love of her has been a valuable and, for some people, an indispensable initiation.

I need not say "has been." For in fact those who allow no more than this to the love of nature seem to be those who retain it. This is what one should expect. This love, when it sets up as a religion, is beginning to be a god—therefore to be a demon. And demons never keep their promises. Nature "dies" on those who try to live for a love of nature. Coleridge ended by being insensible to her; Wordsworth, by lamenting that the glory had passed away. Say your prayers in a garden early, ignoring steadfastly the dew, the birds and the flowers, and you will come away overwhelmed by its freshness and joy; go there in order to be overwhelmed and, after a certain age, nine times out of ten nothing will happen to you.

I turn now to the love of one's country. Here there is no need to labour M. de Rougemont's maxim; we all know now that this love becomes a demon when it becomes a god. Some begin to suspect that it is never anything but a demon. But then they have to reject half the high poetry and half the heroic action our race has achieved. We cannot keep even Christ's lament over Jerusalem. He too exhibits love for His country.

Let us limit our field. There is no need here for an essay on international ethics. When this love becomes demoniac it will of course produce wicked acts. But others, more skilled, may say what acts between nations are wicked. We are only considering the sentiment itself in the hope of being able to distinguish its innocent from its demoniac condition. Neither of these is the efficient cause of national behaviour. For strictly speaking it is rulers, not nations, who behave internationally. Demoniac patriotism in their subjects—I write only for subjects—will make it easier for them to act wickedly; healthy patriotism may make it harder: when they are wicked they may by propaganda encourage a demoniac condition of our sentiments in order to secure our acquiescence in their wickedness. If they are good, they could do the opposite. That is one reason why we private persons should keep a wary eye on the health or disease of our own love for our country. And that is what I am writing about.

How ambivalent patriotism is may be gauged by the fact that no two writers have expressed it more vigorously than Kipling and Chesterton. If it were one element two such men could not both have praised it. In reality it contains many ingredients, of which many different blends are possible.

First, there is love of home, of the place we grew up in or the places, perhaps many, which have been our homes; and of all places fairly near these and fairly like them; love of old acquaintances, of familiar sights, sounds and smells. Note that at its largest this is, for us, a love of England, Wales, Scotland, or Ulster. Only foreigners and politicians talk about "Britain." Kipling's "I do not love my empire's foes" strikes a ludicrously false note. *My* empire! With this love for the place there goes a love for the way of life; for beer and tea and open fires, trains with compartments in them and an unarmed police force and all the rest of it; for the local dialect and (a shade less) for our native language. As Chesterton says, a man's reasons for not wanting his country to be ruled by foreigners are very like his reasons for not wanting his house to be burned down; because he "could not even begin" to enumerate all the things he would miss.

It would be hard to find any legitimate point of view from which this feeling could be condemned. As the family offers us the first step beyond self-love, so this offers us the first step beyond family selfishness. Of course it is not pure charity; it involves love of our neighbours in the local, not of our Neighbour, in the Dominical, sense. But those who do not love the fellow-villagers or fellow-townsmen whom they *have* seen are not likely to have got very far towards loving "Man" whom they have not. All natural affections, including this, can become rivals to spiritual love: but they can also be preparatory imitations of it, training (so to speak) of the spiritual muscles which Grace may later put to a higher service; as women nurse dolls in childhood and later nurse children. There may come an occasion for renouncing this love; pluck out your right eye. But you need to have an eye first: a creature which had none—which had only got so far as a "photo-sensitive" spot—would be very ill employed in meditation on that severe text.

Of course patriotism of this kind is not in the least aggressive. It asks only to be let alone. It becomes militant only to protect what it loves. In any mind which has a pennyworth of imagination it produces a good attitude towards foreigners. How can I love my home without coming to realise that other men, no less rightly, love theirs? Once you have realised that the Frenchmen like *café complet* just as we like bacon and eggs—why, good luck to them and let them have it. The last thing we want is to make everywhere else just like our own home. It would not be home unless it were different.

The second ingredient is a particular attitude to our country's past. I mean to that past as it lives in popular imagination; the great deeds of our ancestors. Remember Marathon. Remember Waterloo. "We must be free or die who speak the tongue that Shakespeare spoke." This past is felt both to impose an obligation and to hold out an assurance; we must not fall below the standard our fathers set us, and because we are their sons there is good hope we shall not.

This feeling has not quite such good credentials as the sheer love of home. The actual history of every country is full of shabby and even shameful doings. The heroic stories, if taken to be typical, give a false impression of it and are often themselves open to serious historical criticism. Hence a patriotism based on our glorious past is fair game for the debunker. As knowledge increases it may snap and be converted into disillusioned cynicism, or may be maintained by a voluntary shutting of the eyes. But who can condemn what clearly makes many people, at many important moments, behave so much better than they could have done without its help?

I think it is possible to be strengthened by the image of the past without being either deceived or puffed up. The image becomes dangerous in the precise degree to which it is mistaken, or substituted, for serious and systematic historical study. The stories are best when they are handed on and accepted as stories. I do not mean by this that they should be handed on as mere fictions (some of them are after all true). But the emphasis should be on the tale as such, on the picture which fires the imagination, the example that strengthens the will. The schoolboy who hears them should dimly feel—though of course he cannot put it into words—that he is hearing *saga*. Let him be thrilled—preferably "out of school"— by the "Deeds that won the Empire"; but the less we mix this up with his "history lessons" or mistake it for a serious analysis—worse still, a justification—of imperial policy, the better. When I was a child I had a book full of coloured pictures called *Our Island Story.* That title has always seemed to me to strike exactly the right note. The book did not look at all like a text-book either. What does seem to me poisonous, what breeds a type of patriotism that is pernicious if it lasts but not likely to last long in an educated adult, is the perfectly serious indoctrination of the young in knowably false or biased history—the heroic legend drably disguised as text-book fact. With this creeps in the tacit assumption that other nations have not equally their heroes; perhaps even the belief—surely it is very bad biology—that we can literally "inherit" a tradition. And these almost inevitably lead on to a third thing that is sometimes called patriotism.

This third thing is not a sentiment but a belief: a firm, even prosaic belief that our own nation, in sober fact, has long been, and still is markedly superior to all others. I once ventured to say to an old clergyman who was voicing this sort of patriotism, "But, sir, aren't we told that *every* people thinks its own men the bravest and its own women the fairest in the world?" He replied with total gravity—he could not have been graver if he had been saying the Creed at the altar—"Yes, but in England it's true." To be sure, this conviction had not made my friend (God rest his soul) a villain; only an extremely lovable old ass. It can however produce asses that kick and bite. On the lunatic fringe it may shade off into that popular Racialism which Christianity and science equally forbid.

This brings us to the fourth ingredient. If our nation is really so much better than others it may be held to have either the duties or the rights of a superior being towards them. In the nineteenth century the English became very conscious of such duties: the "white man's burden." What we called *natives* were our wards and we their self-appointed guardians. This was not all hypocrisy. We did do them some good. But our habit of talking as if England's motives for acquiring an empire (or any youngster's motives for seeking a job in the Indian Civil Service) had been mainly altruistic nauseated the world. And yet this showed the sense of superiority working at its best. Some nations who have also felt it have stressed the rights not the duties. To them, some foreigners were so bad that one had the right to exterminate them. Others, fitted only to be hewers of wood and drawers of water to the chosen people, had better be made to get on with their hewing and drawing. Dogs, know your betters! I am far from suggesting that the two attitudes are on the same level. But both are fatal. Both demand that the area in which they operate should grow "wider still and wider." And both have about them this sure mark of evil: only by being terrible do they avoid being comic. If there were no broken treaties with Redskins, no extermination of the Tasmanians, no gas-chambers and no Belsen, no Amritsar, Black and Tans or Apartheid, the pomposity of both would be roaring farce.

Finally we reach the stage where patriotism in its demoniac form unconsciously denies itself. Chesterton picked on two lines from Kipling as the perfect example. It was unfair to Kipling, who knew—wonderfully, for so homeless a man—what the love of home can mean. But the lines, in isolation, can be taken to sum up the thing. They run:

> *If England was what England seems*
> *'Ow quick we'd drop 'er. But she ain't!*

Love never spoke that way. It is like loving your children only "if they're good," your wife only while she keeps her looks, your husband only so long as he is famous and successful. "No man," said one of the Greeks, "loves his city because it is great, but because it is his." A man who really loves his country will love her in her ruin and degeneration—"England, with all thy faults, I love thee still." She will be to him "a poor thing but mine own." He may think her good and great, when she is not, because he loves her; the delusion is up to a point pardonable. But Kipling's soldier reverses it; he loves her because he thinks her good and great—loves her on her merits. She is a fine going concern and it gratifies his pride to be in it. How if she ceased to be such? The answer is plainly given: " 'Ow quick we'd drop 'er." When the ship begins to sink he will leave her. Thus that kind of patriotism which sets off with the greatest swagger of drums and banners actually sets off on the road that can lead to Vichy. And this is a phenomenon which will meet us again. When the natural loves become lawless they do not merely do harm to other loves; they themselves cease to be the loves they were—to be loves at all.

Patriotism has, then, many faces. Those who would reject it entirely do not seem to have considered what will certainly step—has already begun to step—into its place. For a long time yet, or perhaps forever, nations will live in danger. Rulers must somehow nerve their subjects to defend them or at least to prepare for their defence. Where the sentiment of patriotism has been destroyed this can be done only by presenting every international conflict in a purely ethical light. If people will spend neither sweat nor blood for "their country" they must be made to feel that they are spending them for justice, or civilisation, or humanity. This is a step down, not up. Patriotic sentiment did not of course need to disregard ethics. Good men needed to be convinced that their country's cause was just; but it was still their country's cause, not the cause of justice as such. The difference seems to me important. I may without self-righteousness or hypocrisy think it just to defend my house by force against a burglar; but if I start pretending that I blacked his eye purely on moral grounds—wholly indifferent to the fact that the house in question was mine—I become insufferable. The pretence that when England's cause is just we are on England's side—as some neutral Don Quixote might be—for that reason alone, is equally spurious. And nonsense draws evil after it. If our country's cause is the cause of God, wars must be wars of annihilation. A false transcendence is given to things which are very much of this world.

The glory of the old sentiment was that while it could steel men to the utmost endeavour, it still knew itself to be a sentiment. Wars could be heroic without pretending to be Holy Wars. The hero's death was not confused with the martyr's. And (delightfully) the same sentiment which could be so serious in a rear-guard action could also in peacetime take itself as lightly as all happy loves often do. It could laugh at itself. Our older patriotic songs cannot be sung without a twinkle in the eye; later ones sound more like hymns. Give me "The British Grenadiers" (*with a tow-row-row-row*) any day rather than "Land of Hope and Glory."

It will be noticed that the sort of love I have been describing, and all its ingredients, can be for something other than a country: for a school, a regiment, a great family, or a class. All the same criticisms will still apply. It can also be felt for bodies that claim more than a natural affection: for a Church or (alas) a party in a Church, or for a religious order. This terrible subject would require a book to itself. Here it will be enough to say that the Heavenly Society is also an earthly society. Our (merely natural) patriotism towards the latter can very easily borrow the transcendent claims of the former and use them to justify the most abominable actions. If ever the book which I am not going to write is written it must be the full confession by Christendom of Christendom's specific contribution to the sum of human cruelty and treachery. Large areas of "the World" will not hear us till we have publicly disowned much of our past. Why should they? We have shouted the name of Christ and enacted the service of Moloch.

It may be thought that I should not end this chapter without a word about our love for animals. But that will fit in better in the next. Whether animals are in fact sub-personal or not, they are never loved as if they were. The fact or the illusion of personality is always present, so that love for them is really an instance of that Affection which is the subject of the following chapter.

AFFECTION

I begin with the humblest and most widely diffused of loves, the love in which our experience seems to differ least from that of the animals. Let me add at once that I do not on that account give it a lower value. Nothing in Man is either worse or better for being shared with the beasts. When we blame a man for being "a mere animal," we mean not that he displays animal characteristics (we all do) but that he displays these, and only these, on occasions where the specifically human was demanded. (When we call him "brutal" we usually mean that he commits cruelties impossible to most real brutes; they're not clever enough.)

The Greeks called this love *storge* (two syllables and the g is "hard"). I shall here call it simply Affection. My Greek Lexicon defines *storge* as "affection, especially of parents to offspring"; but also of offspring to parents. And that, I have no doubt, is the original form of the thing as well as the central meaning of the word. The image we must start with is that of a mother nursing a baby; a bitch or a cat with a basketful of puppies or kittens; all in a squeaking, nuzzling heap together; purrings, lickings, baby-talk, milk, warmth, the smell of young life.

The importance of this image is that it presents us at the very outset with a certain paradox. The Need and Need-love of the young is obvious; so is the Gift-love of the mother. She gives birth, gives suck, gives protection. On the other hand, she must give birth or die. She must give suck or suffer. That way, her Affection too is a Need-love. There is the paradox. It is a Need-love but what it needs is to give. It is a Gift-love but it needs to be needed. We shall have to return to this point.

But even in animal life, and still more in our own, Affection extends far beyond the relation of mother and young. This warm comfortableness, this satisfaction in being together, takes in all sorts of objects. It is indeed the least discriminating of loves. There are women for whom we can predict few wooers and men who are likely to have few friends. They have nothing to offer. But almost anyone can become an object of Affection; the ugly, the stupid, even the exasperating. There need be no apparent fitness between those whom it unites. I have seen it felt for an imbecile not only by his parents but by his brothers. It ignores the barriers of age, sex, class and education. It can exist between a clever young man from the university and an old nurse, though their minds inhabit different worlds. It ignores even the barriers of species. We see it not only between dog and man but, more surprisingly, between dog and cat. Gilbert White claims to have discovered it between a horse and a hen.

Some of the novelists have seized this well. In *Tristram Shandy* "My Father" and Uncle Toby are so far from being united by any community of interests or ideas that they cannot converse for ten minutes without cross-purposes; but we are made to feel their deep mutual affection. So with Don Quixote and Sancho Panza, Pickwick and Sam Weller, Dick Swiveller and the Marchioness. So too, though probably without the author's conscious intention, in *The Wind in the Willows;* the quaternion of Mole, Rat, Badger, and Toad suggests the amazing heterogeneity possible between those who are bound by Affection.

But Affection has its own criteria. Its objects have to be familiar. We can sometimes point to the very day and hour when we fell in love or began a new friendship. I doubt if we ever catch Affection beginning. To become aware of it is to become aware that it has already been going on for some time. The use of "old" or *vieux* as a term of Affection is significant. The dog barks at strangers who have never done it any harm and wags its tail for old acquaintances even if they never did it a good turn. The child will love a crusty old gardener who has hardly ever taken any notice of it and shrink from the visitor who is making every attempt to win its regard. But it must be an *old* gardener, one who has "always" been there—the short but seemingly immemorial "always" of childhood.

Affection, as I have said, is the humblest love. It gives itself no airs. People can be proud of being "in love," or of friendship. Affection is modest—even furtive and shame-faced. Once when I had remarked on the affection quite often found between cat and dog, my friend replied, "Yes. But I bet no dog would ever confess it to the other dogs." That is at least a good caricature of much human Affection. "Let homely faces stay at home," says Comus. Now Affection has a very homely face. So have many of those for whom we feel it. It is no proof of our refinement or perceptiveness that we love them; nor that they love us. What I have called Appreciative love is no basic element in Affection. It usually needs absence or bereavement to set us praising those to whom only Affection binds us. We take them for granted: and this taking for granted, which is an outrage in erotic love, is here right and proper up to a point. It fits the comfortable, quiet nature of the feeling. Affection would not be affection if it was loudly and frequently expressed; to produce it in public is like getting your household furniture out for a move. It did very well in its place, but it looks shabby or tawdry or grotesque in the sunshine. Affection almost slinks or seeps through our lives. It lives with humble un-dress, private things; soft slippers, old clothes, old jokes, the thump of a sleepy dog's tail on the kitchen floor, the sound of a sewing-machine, a gollywog left on the lawn.

But I must at once correct myself. I am talking of Affection as it is when it exists apart from the other loves. It often does so exist; often not. As gin is not only a drink in itself but also a base for many mixed drinks, so Affection, besides being a love itself, can enter into the other loves and colour them all through and become the very medium in which from day to day they operate. They would not perhaps wear very well without it. To make a friend is not the same as to become affectionate. But when your friend has become an old friend, all those things about him which had originally nothing to do with the friendship become familiar and dear with familiarity. As for erotic love, I can imagine nothing more disagreeable than to experience it for more than a very short time without this homespun clothing of affection. That would be a most uneasy condition, either too angelic or too animal or each by turn; never quite great enough or little enough for man. There is indeed a peculiar charm, both in friendship and in Eros, about those moments when Appreciative love lies, as it were, curled up asleep, and the mere ease and ordinariness of the relationship (free as solitude, yet neither is alone) wraps us round. No need to talk. No need to make love. No needs at all except perhaps to stir the fire.

This blending and overlapping of the loves is well kept before us by the fact that at most times and places all three of them had in common, as their expression, the kiss. In modern England friendship no longer uses it, but Affection and Eros do. It belongs so fully to both that we cannot now tell which borrowed it from the other or whether there were borrowing at all. To be sure, you may say that the kiss of Affection differs from the kiss of Eros. Yes; but not all kisses between lovers are lovers' kisses. Again, both these loves tend—and it embarrasses many moderns—to use a "little language" or "baby talk." And this is not peculiar to the human species. Professor Lorenz has told us that when jackdaws are amorous their calls "consist chiefly of infantile sounds reserved by adult jackdaws for these occasions" (*King Solomon's Ring*, p. 158). We and the birds have the same excuse. Different sorts of tenderness are both tenderness and the language of the earliest tenderness we have ever known is recalled to do duty for the new sort.

One of the most remarkable by-products of Affection has not yet been mentioned. I have said that is not primarily an Appreciative love. It is not discriminating. It can "rub along" with the most unpromising people. Yet oddly enough this very fact means that it can in the end make appreciations possible which, but for it, might never have existed. We may say, and not quite untruly, that we have chosen our friends and the woman we love for their various excellences—for beauty, frankness, goodness of heart, wit, intelligence, or what not. But it had to be the particular kind of wit, the particular kind of beauty, the particular kind of goodness that we like, and we have our personal tastes in these matters. That is why friends and lovers feel that they were "made for one another." The especial glory of Affection is that it can unite those who most emphatically, even comically, are not; people who, if they had not found themselves put down by fate in the same household or community, would have had nothing to do with each other. If Affection grows out of this—of course it often does not— their eyes begin to open. Growing fond of "old so-and-so," at first simply because he happens to be there, I presently begin to see that there is "something in him" after all. The moment when one first says, really meaning it, that though he is not "my sort of man" he is a very good man "in his own way" is one of liberation. It does not feel like that; we may feel only tolerant and indulgent. But really we have crossed a frontier. That "in his own way" means that we are getting beyond our own idiosyncrasies, that we are learning to appreciate goodness or intelligence in themselves, not merely goodness or intelligence flavoured and served to suit our own palate.

"Dogs and cats should always be brought up together," said someone, "it broadens their minds so."

Affection broadens ours; of all natural loves it is the most catholic, the least finical, the broadest. The people with whom you are thrown together in the family, the college, the mess, the ship, the religious house, are from this point of view a wider circle than the friends, however numerous, whom you have made for yourself in the outer world. By having a great many friends I do not prove that I have a wide appreciation of human excellence. You might as well say I prove the width of my literary taste by being able to enjoy all the books in my own study. The answer is the same in both cases—"You chose those books. You chose those friends. Of course they suit you." The truly wide taste in reading is that which enables a man to find something for his needs on the sixpenny tray outside any secondhand bookshop. The truly wide taste in humanity will similarly find something to appreciate in the cross-section of humanity whom one has to meet every day. In my experience it is Affection that creates this taste, teaching us first to notice, then to endure, then to smile at, then to enjoy, and finally to appreciate, the people who "happen to be there." Made for us? Thank God, no. They are themselves, odder than you could have believed and worth far more than we guessed.

And now we are drawing near the point of danger. Affection, I have said, gives itself no airs; charity, said St. Paul, is not puffed up. Affection can love the unattractive: God and His saints love the unlovable. Affection "does not expect too much," turns a blind eye to faults, revives easily after quarrels; just so charity suffers long and is kind and forgives. Affection opens our eyes to goodness we could not have seen, or should not have appreciated without it. So does humble sanctity. If we dwelled exclusively on these resemblances we might be led on to believe that this Affection is not simply one of the natural loves but is Love Himself working in our human hearts and fulfilling the law. Were the Victorian novelists right after all? Is love (of this sort) really enough? Are the "domestic affections," when in their best and fullest development, the same thing as the Christian life? The answer to all these questions, I submit, is certainly No.

I do not mean simply that those novelists sometimes wrote as if they had never heard the text about "hating" wife and mother and one's own life also. That of course is true. The rivalry between all natural loves and the love of God is something a Christian dare not forget. God is the great Rival, the ultimate object of human jealousy; that beauty, terrible as the Gorgon's, which may at any moment steal from me—or it seems like stealing to me—my wife's or husband's or daughter's heart. The bitterness of some unbelief, though disguised even from those who feel it as anti-clericalism or hatred of superstition, is really due to this. But I am not at present thinking of that rivalry; we shall have to face it in a later chapter. For the moment our business is more down to earth.

How many of these "happy homes" really exist? Worse still; are all the unhappy ones unhappy because Affection is absent? I believe not. It can be present, causing the unhappiness. Nearly all the characteristics of this love are ambivalent. They may work for ill as well as for good. By itself, left simply to follow its own bent, it can darken and degrade human life. The debunkers and anti-sentimentalists have not said all the truth about it, but all they have said is true.

Symptomatic of this, perhaps, is the odiousness of nearly all those treacly tunes and saccharine poems in which popular art expresses Affection. They are odious because of their falsity. They represent as a ready-made recipe for bliss (and even for goodness) what is in fact only an opportunity. There is no hint that we shall have to do anything: only let Affection pour over us like a warm shower-bath and all, it is implied, will be well.

Affection, we have seen, includes both Need-love and Gift-love. I begin with the Need—our craving for the Affection of others.

Now there is a clear reason why this craving, of all love-cravings, easily becomes the most unreasonable. I have said that almost anyone may be the object of Affection. Yes; and almost everyone expects to be. The egregious Mr. Pontifex in *The Way of All Flesh* is outraged to discover that his son does not love him; it is "unnatural" for a boy not to love his own father. It never occurs to him to ask whether, since the first day the boy can remember, he has ever done or said anything that could excite love. Similarly, at the beginning of *King Lear* the hero is shown as a very unlovable old man devoured with a ravenous appetite for Affection. I am driven to literary examples because you, the reader, and I do not live in the same neighbourhood; if we did, there would unfortunately be no difficulty about replacing them with examples from real life. The thing happens every day. And we can see why. We all know that we must do something, if not to merit, at least to attract, erotic love or friendship. But Affection is often assumed to be provided, ready made, by nature; "built-in," "laid-on," "on the house." We have a right to expect it. If the others do not give it, they are "unnatural."

This assumption is no doubt the distortion of a truth. Much has been "built-in." Because we are a mammalian species, instinct will provide at least some degree, often a high one, of maternal love. Because we are a social species familiar association provides a *milieu* in which, if all goes well, Affection will arise and grow strong without demanding any very shining qualities in its objects. If it is given us it will not necessarily be given us on our merits; we may get it with very little trouble. From a dim perception of the truth (many are loved with Affection far beyond their deserts) Mr. Pontifex draws the ludicrous conclusion, "Therefore I, without desert, have a right to it." It is as if, on a far higher plane, we argued that because no man by merit has a right to the Grace of God, I, having no merit, am entitled to it. There is no question of rights in either case. What we have is not "a right to expect" but a "reasonable expectation" of being loved by our intimates if we, and they, are more or less ordinary people. But we may not be. We may be intolerable. If we are, "nature" will work against us. For the very same conditions of intimacy which make Affection possible also—and no less naturally—make possible a peculiarly incurable distaste; a hatred as immemorial, constant, unemphatic, almost at times unconscious, as the corresponding form of love. Siegfried, in the opera, could not remember a time before every shuffle, mutter, and fidget of his dwarfish foster-father had become odious. We never catch this kind of hatred, any more than Affection, at the moment of its beginning. It was always there before. Notice that *old* is a term of wearied loathing as well as of endearment: "at his old tricks," "in his old way," "the same old thing."

It would be absurd to say that Lear is lacking in Affection. In so far as Affection is Need-love he is half-crazy with it. Unless, in his own way, he loved his daughters he would not so desperately desire their love. The most unlovable parent (or child) may be full of such ravenous love. But it works to their own misery and everyone else's. The situation becomes suffocating. If people are already unlovable a continual demand on their part (as of right) to be loved—their manifest sense of injury, their reproaches, whether loud and clamorous or merely implicit in every look and gesture of resentful self-pity—produce in us a sense of guilt (they are intended to do so) for a fault we could not have avoided and cannot cease to commit. They seal up the very fountain for which they are thirsty. If ever, at some favoured moment, any germ of Affection for them stirs in us, their demand for more and still more petrifies us again. And of course such people always desire the same proof of our love; we are to join their side, to hear and share their grievance against someone else. If my boy really loved me he would see how selfish his father is . . . if my brother loved me he would make a party with me against my sister . . . if you loved me you wouldn't let me be treated like this . . .

And all the while they remain unaware of the real road. "If you would be loved, be lovable," said Ovid. That cheery old reprobate only meant, "If you want to attract the girls you must be attractive," but his maxim has a wider application. The amorist was wiser in his generation than Mr. Pontifex and King Lear.

The really surprising thing is not that these insatiable demands made by the unlovable are sometimes made in vain, but that they are so often met. Sometimes one sees a woman's girlhood, youth and long years of her maturity up to the verge of old age all spent in tending, obeying, caressing, and perhaps supporting, a maternal vampire who can never be caressed and obeyed enough. The sacrifice—but there are two opinions about that—may be beautiful; the old woman who exacts it is not.

The "built-in" or unmerited character of Affection thus invites a hideous misinterpretation. So does its ease and informality.

We hear a great deal about the rudeness of the rising generation. I am an oldster myself and might be expected to take the oldsters' side, but in fact I have been far more impressed by the bad manners of parents to children than by those of children to parents. Who has not been the embarrassed guest at family meals where the father or mother treated their grown-up offspring with an incivility which, offered to any other young people, would simply have terminated the acquaintance? Dogmatic assertions on matters which the children understand and their elders don't, ruthless interruptions, flat contradictions, ridicule of things the young take seriously—sometimes of their religion—insulting references to their friends, all provide an easy answer to the question "Why are they always out? Why do they like every house better than their home?" Who does not prefer civility to barbarism?

If you asked any of these insufferable people—they are not all parents of course—why they behaved that way at home, they would reply, "Oh, hang it all, one comes home to relax. A chap can't be always on his best behaviour. If a man can't be himself in his own house, where can he? Of course we don't want Company Manners at home. We're a happy family. We can say *anything* to one another here. No one minds. We all understand."

Once again it is so nearly true yet so fatally wrong. Affection is an affair of old clothes, and ease, of the unguarded moment, of liberties which would be ill-bred if we took them with strangers. But old clothes are one thing; to wear the same shirt till it stank would be another. There are proper clothes for a garden party; but the clothes for home must be proper too, in their own different way. Similarly there is a distinction between public and domestic courtesy. The root principle of both is the same: "that no one give any kind of preference to himself." But the more public the occasion, the more our obedience to this principle has been "taped" or formalised. There are "rules" of good manners. The more intimate the occasion, the less the formalisation; but not therefore the less need of courtesy. On the contrary, Affection at its best practises a courtesy which is incomparably more subtle, sensitive, and deep than the public kind. In public a ritual would do. At home you must have the reality which that ritual represented, or else the deafening triumphs of the greatest egoist present. You must really give no kind of preference to yourself; at a party it is enough to conceal the preference. Hence the old proverb "come live with me and you'll know me." Hence a man's familiar manners first reveal the true value of his (significantly odious phrase!) "Company" or "Party" manners. Those who leave their manners behind them when they come home from the dance or the sherry party have no real courtesy even there. They were merely aping those who had.

"We can say *anything* to one another." The truth

43

behind this is that Affection at its best can say whatever Affection at its best wishes to say, regardless of the rules that govern public courtesy; for Affection at its best wishes neither to wound nor to humiliate nor to domineer. You may address the wife of your bosom as "Pig!" when she has inadvertently drunk your cocktail as well as her own. You may roar down the story which your father is telling once too often. You may tease and hoax and banter. You can say "Shut up. I want to read." You can do anything in the right tone and at the right moment—the tone and moment which are not intended to, and will not, hurt. The better the Affection the more unerringly it knows which these are (every love has its *art of love*). But the domestic Rudesby means something quite different when he claims liberty to say "anything." Having a very imperfect sort of Affection himself, or perhaps at that moment none, he arrogates to himself the beautiful liberties which only the fullest Affection has a right to or knows how to manage. He then uses them spitefully in obedience to his resentments; or ruthlessly in obedience to his egoism; or at best stupidly, lacking the art. And all the time he may have a clear conscience. He knows that Affection takes liberties. He is taking liberties. Therefore (he concludes) he is being affectionate. Resent anything and he will say that the defect of love is on your side. He is hurt. He has been misunderstood.

He then sometimes avenges himself by getting on his high horse and becoming elaborately "polite." The implication is of course, "Oh! So we are not to be intimate? We are to behave like mere acquaintances? I had hoped—but no matter. Have it your own way." This illustrates prettily the difference between intimate and formal courtesy. Precisely what suits the one may be a breach of the other. To be free and easy when you are presented to some eminent stranger is bad manners; to practise formal and ceremonial courtesies at home ("public faces in private places") is—and is always intended to be—bad manners. There is a delicious illustration of really good domestic manners in *Tristram Shandy*. At a singularly unsuitable moment Uncle Toby has been holding forth on his favourite theme of fortification. "My Father," driven for once beyond endurance, violently interrupts. Then he sees his brother's face; the utterly unretaliating face of Toby, deeply wounded, not by the slight to himself—he would never think of that—but by the slight to the noble art. "My Father" at once repents. There is an apology, a total reconciliation. Uncle Toby, to show how complete is his forgiveness, to show that he is not on his dignity, resumes the lecture on fortification.

But we have not yet touched on jealousy. I suppose no one now believes that jealousy is especially connected with erotic love. If anyone does, the behaviour of children, employees, and domestic animals ought soon to undeceive him. Every kind of love, almost every kind of association, is liable to it. The jealousy of Affection is closely connected with its reliance on what is old and familiar. So also with the total, or relative, unimportance for Affection of what I call Appreciative love. We don't want the "old, familiar faces" to become brighter or more beautiful, the old ways to be changed even for the better, the old jokes and interests to be replaced by exciting novelties. Change is a threat to Affection.

A brother and sister, or two brothers—for sex here is not at work—grow to a certain age sharing everything.

They have read the same comics, climbed the same trees, been pirates or spacemen together, taken up and abandoned stamp-collecting at the same moment. Then a dreadful thing happens. One of them flashes ahead—discovers poetry or science or serious music or perhaps undergoes a religious conversion. His life is flooded with the new interest. The other cannot share it; he is left behind. I doubt whether even the infidelity of a wife or husband raises a more miserable sense of desertion or a fiercer jealousy than this can sometimes do. It is not yet jealousy of the new friends whom the deserter will soon be making. That will come; at first it is jealousy of the thing itself—of this science, this music, of God (always called "religion" or "all this religion" in such contexts). The jealousy will probably be expressed by ridicule. The new interest is "all silly nonsense," contemptibly childish (or contemptibly grown-up), or else the deserter is not really interested in it at all—he's showing off, swanking; it's all affectation. Presently the books will be hidden, the scientific specimens destroyed, the radio forcibly switched off the classical programmes. For Affection is the most instinctive, in that sense the most animal, of the loves; its jealousy is proportionately fierce. It snarls and bares its teeth like a dog whose food has been snatched away. And why would it not? Something or someone has snatched away from the child I am picturing his life-long food, his second self. His world is in ruins.

But it is not only children who react thus. Few things in the ordinary peacetime life of a civilised country are more nearly fiendish than the rancour with which a whole unbelieving family will turn on the one member of it who has become a Christian, or a whole low-brow family on the one who shows signs of becoming an intellectual. This is not, as I once thought, simply the innate and, as it were, disinterested hatred of darkness for light. A church-going family in which one has gone atheist will not always behave any better. It is the reaction to a desertion, even to robbery. Someone or something has stolen "our" boy (or girl). He who was one of Us has become one of Them. What right had anybody to do it? He is *ours*. But once change has thus begun, who knows where it will end? (And we all so happy and comfortable before and doing no harm to no one!)

Sometimes a curious double jealousy is felt, or rather two inconsistent jealousies which chase each other round in the sufferer's mind. On the one hand "This" is "All nonsense, all bloody high-brow nonsense, all canting humbug." But on the other, "Supposing—it can't be, it mustn't be, but just supposing—there were something in it?" Supposing there really were anything in literature, or in Christianity? How if the deserter has really entered a new world which the rest of us never suspected? But, if so, how unfair! Why him? Why was it never opened to us? "A chit of a girl—a whipper-snapper of a boy— being shown things that are hidden from their elders?" And since that is clearly incredible and unendurable, jealousy returns to the hypothesis "All nonsense."

Parents in this state are much more comfortably placed than brothers and sisters. Their past is unknown to their children. Whatever the deserter's new world is, they can always claim that they have been through it themselves and come out the other end. "It's a phase," they say. "It'll blow over." Nothing could be more satisfactory. It cannot be there and then refuted, for it is a statement about the future. It stings, yet—so indulgently said—is hard to resent. Better still, the elders may really believe it. Best of all, it may finally turn out to have been true. It won't be their fault if it doesn't.

"Boy, boy, these wild courses of yours will break your mother's heart." That eminently Victorian appeal may often have been true. Affection was bitterly wounded when one member of the family fell from the homely *ethos* into something worse—gambling, drink, keeping an opera girl. Unfortunately it is almost equally possible to break your mother's heart by rising above the homely *ethos*. The conservative tenacity of Affection works both ways. It can be a domestic counterpart to that nationally suicidal type of education which keeps back the promising child because the idlers and dunces might be "hurt" if it were undemocratically moved into a higher class than themselves.

All these perversions of Affection are mainly connected with Affection as a Need-love. But Affection as a Gift-love has its perversions too.

I am thinking of Mrs. Fidget, who died a few months ago. It is really astonishing how her family have brightened up. The drawn look has gone from her husband's face; he begins to be able to laugh. The younger boy, whom I had always thought an embittered, peevish little creature, turns out to be quite human. The elder, who was hardly ever at home except when he was in bed, is nearly always there now and has begun to reorganise the garden. The girl, who was always supposed to be "delicate" (though I never found out what exactly the trouble was), now has the riding lessons which were once out of the question, dances all night, and plays any amount of tennis. Even the dog who was never allowed out except on a lead is now a well-known member of the Lamp-post Club in their road.

Mrs. Fidget very often said that she lived for her family. And it was not untrue. Everyone in the neighbourhood knew it. "She lives for her family," they said; "what a wife and mother!" She did all the washing; true, she did it badly, and they could have afforded to send it out to a laundry, and they frequently begged her not to do it. But she did. There was always a hot lunch for anyone who was at home and always a hot meal at night (even in midsummer). They implored her not to provide this. They protested almost with tears in their eyes (and with truth) that they liked cold meals. It made no difference. She was living for her family. She always sat up to "welcome" you home if you were out late at night; two or three in the morning, it made no odds; you would always find the frail, pale, weary face awaiting you, like a silent accusation. Which meant of course that you couldn't with any decency go out very often. She was always making things too; being in her own estimation (I'm no judge myself) an excellent amateur dressmaker and a great knitter. And of course, unless you were a heartless brute, you had to wear the things. (The Vicar tells me that, since her death, the contributions of that family alone to "sales of work" outweigh those of all his other parishioners put together.) And then her care for their health! She bore the whole burden of that daughter's "delicacy" alone. The Doctor—an old friend, and it was not being done on National Health—was never allowed to discuss matters with his patient. After the briefest examination of her, he was taken into another room by the mother. The girl was to have no worries, no responsibility for her own health. Only loving care; caresses, special foods, horrible tonic wines, and breakfast in bed. For Mrs. Fidget, as she so often said, would "work her fingers to the bone" for her family. They couldn't stop her. Nor could they—being decent people—quite sit still and watch her do it. They had to help. Indeed they were always having to help. That is, they did things for her to help her to do things for them which they didn't want done. As for the dear dog, it was to her, she said, "Just like one of the children." It was in fact, as like one of them as she could make it. But since it had no scruples it got on rather better than they, and though vetted, dieted and guarded within an inch of its life, contrived sometimes to reach the dustbin or the dog next door.

The Vicar says Mrs. Fidget is now at rest. Let us hope she is. What's quite certain is that her family are.

It is easy to see how liability to this state is, so to speak, congenital in the maternal instinct. This, as we saw, is a Gift-love, but one that needs to give; therefore needs to be needed. But the proper aim of giving is to put the recipient in a state where he no longer needs our gift. We feed children in order that they may soon be able to feed themselves; we teach them in order that they may soon not need our teaching. Thus a heavy task is laid upon this Gift-love. It must work towards its own abdication. We must aim at making ourselves superfluous. The hour when we can say "They need me no longer" should be our reward. But the instinct, simply in its own nature, has no power to fulfil this law. The instinct desires the good of its object, but not simply; only the good it can itself give. A much higher love—a love which desires the good of the object as such, from whatever source that good comes—must step in and help or tame the instinct before it can make the abdication. And of course it often does. But where it does not, the ravenous need to be needed will gratify itself either by keeping its objects needy or by inventing for them imaginary needs. It will do this all the more ruthlessly because it thinks (in one sense truly) that it is a Gift-love and therefore regards itself as "unselfish."

It is not only mothers who can do this. All those other Affections which, whether by derivation from parental instinct or by similarity of function, need to be needed may fall into the same pit. The Affection of patron for *protégé* is one. In Jane Austen's novel, Emma intends that Harriet Smith should have a happy life; but only the sort of happy life which Emma herself has planned for her. My own profession—that of a university teacher—is in this way dangerous. If we are any good we must always be working towards the moment at which our pupils are fit to become our critics and rivals. We should be delighted when it arrives, as the fencing master is delighted when his pupil can pink and disarm him. And many are.

But not all. I am old enough to remember the sad case of Dr. Quartz. No university boasted a more effective or devoted teacher. He spent the whole of himself on his pupils. He made an indelible impression on nearly all of them. He was the object of much well-merited hero-worship. Naturally, and delightfully, they continued to visit him after the tutorial relation had ended—went round to his house of an evening and had famous discussions. But the curious thing is that this never lasted. Sooner or later—it might be within a few months or even a few weeks—came the fatal evening when they knocked on his door and were told that the Doctor was engaged. After that he would always be engaged. They were banished from him forever. This was because, at their last meeting, they had rebelled. They had asserted their independence—differed from the master and supported their own view, perhaps not without success. Faced with that very independence which he had laboured to produce and which it was his duty to produce if he could, Dr. Quartz could not bear it. Wotan had toiled to create the free Siegfried; presented with the free Siegfried, he was enraged. Dr. Quartz was an unhappy man.

This terrible need to be needed often finds its outlet in pampering an animal. To learn that someone is "fond of animals" tells us very little until we know in what way. For there are two ways. On the one hand the higher and domesticated animal is, so to speak, a "bridge" between us and the rest of nature. We all at times feel somewhat painfully our human isolation from the subhuman world—the atrophy of instinct which our intelligence entails, our excessive self-consciousness, the innumerable complexities of our situation, our inability to live in the present. If only we could shuffle it all off! We must not—and incidentally we can't—become beasts. But we can be *with* a beast. It is personal enough to give the word *with* a real meaning; yet it remains very largely an unconscious little bundle of biological impulses. It has three legs in nature's world and one in ours. It is a link, an ambassador. Who would not wish, as Bosanquet put it, "to have a representative at the court of Pan"? Man with dog closes a gap in the universe. But of course animals are often used in a worse fashion. If you need to be needed and if your family, very properly, decline to need you, a pet is the obvious substitute. You can keep it all its life in need of you. You can keep it permanently infantile, reduce it to permanent invalidism, cut it off from all genuine animal well-being, and compensate for this by creating needs for countless little indulgences which only you can grant. The unfortunate creature thus becomes very useful to the rest of the household; it acts as a sump or drain—you are too busy spoiling a dog's life to spoil theirs. Dogs are better for this purpose than cats: a monkey, I am told, is best of all. Also it is more like the real thing. To be sure, it's all very bad luck for the animal. But probably it cannot fully realise the wrong you have done it. Better still, you would never know if it did. The most down-trodden human, driven too far, may one day turn and blurt out a terrible truth. Animals can't speak.

Those who say "The more I see of men the better I like dogs"—those who find in animals a *relief* from the demands of human companionship—will be well advised to examine their real reasons.

I hope I am not being misunderstood. If this chapter leads anyone to doubt that the lack of "natural affection" is an extreme depravity I shall have failed. Nor do I question for a moment that Affection is responsible for nine-tenths of whatever solid and durable happiness there is in our natural lives. I shall therefore have some sympathy with those whose comment on the last few pages takes the form "Of course. Of course. These things do happen. Selfish or neurotic people can twist anything, even love, into some sort of misery or exploitation. But why stress these marginal cases? A little common sense, a little give and take, prevents their occurrence among decent people." But I think this comment itself needs a commentary.

Firstly, as to *neurotic*. I do not think we shall see things more clearly by classifying all these malefical states of Affection as pathological. No doubt there are really pathological conditions which make the temptation to these states abnormally hard or even impossible to resist for particular people. Send those people to the doctors by all means. But I believe that everyone who is honest with himself will admit that he has felt these temptations. Their occurrence is not a disease; or if it is, the name of that disease is Being a Fallen Man. In ordinary people the yielding to them—and who does not sometimes yield?—is not disease, but sin. Spiritual direction will here help us more than medical treatment. Medicine labours to restore "natural" structure or "normal" function. But greed, egoism, self-deception and self-pity are not unnatural or abnormal in the same sense as astigmatism or a floating kidney. For who, in Heaven's name, would describe as natural or normal the man from whom these failings were wholly absent? "Natural," if you like, in a quite different sense; archnatural, unfallen. We have seen only one such Man. And He was not at all like the psychologist's picture of the integrated, balanced, adjusted, happily married, employed, popular citizen. You can't really be very well "adjusted" to your world if it says you "have a devil" and ends by nailing you up naked to a stake of wood.

But secondly, the comment in its own language admits the very thing I am trying to say. Affection produces happiness if—and only if—there is common sense and give and take and "decency." In other words, only if something more, and other, than Affection is added. The mere feeling is not enough. You need "common sense," that is, reason. You need "give and take"; that is, you need justice, continually stimulating mere Affection when it fades and restraining it when it forgets or would defy the *art* of love. You need "decency." There is no disguising the fact that this means goodness; patience, self-denial, humility, and the continual intervention of a far higher sort of love than Affection, in itself, can ever be. That is the whole point. If we try to live by Affection alone, Affection will "go bad on us."

How bad, I believe we seldom recognise. Can Mrs. Fidget really have been quite unaware of the countless frustrations and miseries she inflicted on her family? It passes belief. She knew—of course she knew—that it spoiled your whole evening to know that when you came home you would find her uselessly, accusingly, "sitting up for you." She continued all these practices because if she had dropped them she would have been faced with the fact she was determined not to see; would have known that she was not necessary. That is the first motive. Then too, the very laboriousness of her life silenced her secret doubts as to the quality of her love. The more her feet burned and her back ached, the better, for this pain whispered in her ear "How much I must love them if I do all this!" That is the second motive. But I think there is a lower depth. The unappreciativeness of the others, those terrible, wounding words—anything will "wound" a Mrs. Fidget—in which they begged her to send the washing out, enabled her to feel ill-used, therefore, to have a continual grievance, to enjoy the pleasures of resentment. If anyone says he does not know those pleasures, he is a liar or a saint. It is true that they are pleasures only to those who hate. But then a love like Mrs. Fidget's contains a good deal of hatred. It was of erotic love that the Roman poet said, "I love and hate," but other kinds of love admit the same mixture. They carry in them the seeds of hatred. If Affection is made the absolute sovereign of a human life the seeds will germinate. Love, having become a god, becomes a demon.

FRIENDSHIP

When either Affection or Eros is one's theme, one finds
a prepared audience. The importance and beauty of both
have been stressed and almost exaggerated again and
again. Even those who would debunk them are in conscious reaction against this laudatory tradition and, to
that extent, influenced by it. But very few modern people
think Friendship a love of comparable value or even a
love at all. I cannot remember that any poem since *In
Memoriam*, or any novel, has celebrated it. Tristan and
Isolde, Antony and Cleopatra, Romeo and Juliet, have
innumerable counterparts in modern literature: David
and Jonathan, Pylades and Orestes, Roland and Oliver,
Amis and Amile, have not. To the Ancients, Friendship
seemed the happiest and most fully human of all loves;
the crown of life and the school of virtue. The modern
world, in comparison, ignores it. We admit of course
that besides a wife and family a man needs a few

"friends." But the very tone of the admission, and the sort of acquaintanceships which those who make it would describe as "friendships," show clearly that what they are talking about has very little to do with that *Philia* which Aristotle classified among the virtues or that *Amicitia* on which Cicero wrote a book. It is something quite marginal; not a main course in life's banquet; a diversion; something that fills up the chinks of one's time. How has this come about?

The first and most obvious answer is that few value it because few experience it. And the possibility of going through life without the experience is rooted in that fact which separates Friendship so sharply from both the other loves. Friendship is—in a sense not at all derogatory to it—the least *natural* of loves; the least instinctive, organic, biological, gregarious and necessary. It has least commerce with our nerves; there is nothing throaty about it; nothing that quickens the pulse or turns you red and pale. It is essentially between individuals; the moment two men are friends they have in some degree drawn apart together from the herd. Without Eros none of us would have been begotten and without Affection none of us would have been reared; but we can live and breed without Friendship. The species, biologically considered, has no need of it. The pack or herd—the community—may even dislike and distrust it. Its leaders very often do. Headmasters and Headmistresses and Heads of religious communities, colonels and ships' captains, can feel uneasy when close and strong friendships arise between little knots of their subjects.

This (so to call it) "non-natural" quality in Friendship goes far to explain why it was exalted in ancient and medieval times and has come to be made light of in our own. The deepest and most permanent thought of those ages was ascetic and world-renouncing. Nature and emotion and the body were feared as dangers to our souls, or despised as degradations of our human status. Inevitably that sort of love was most prized which seemed most independent, or even defiant, of mere nature. Affection and Eros were too obviously connected with our nerves, too obviously shared with the brutes. You could feel these tugging at your guts and fluttering in your diaphragm. But in Friendship—in that luminous, tranquil, rational world of relationships freely chosen—you got away from all that. This alone, of all the loves, seemed to raise you to the level of gods or angels.

But then came Romanticism and "tearful comedy" and the "return to nature" and the exaltation of Sentiment; and in their train all that great wallow of emotion which, though often criticised, has lasted ever since. Finally, the exaltation of instinct, the dark gods in the blood; whose hierophants may be incapable of male friendship. Under this new dispensation all that had once commended this love now began to work against it. It had not tearful smiles and keepsakes and baby-talk enough to please the sentimentalists. There was not blood and guts enough about it to attract the primitivists. It looked thin and etiolated; a sort of vegetarian substitute for the more organic loves.

Other causes have contributed. To those—and they are now the majority—who see human life merely as a development and complication of animal life all forms of behaviour which cannot produce certificates of an animal origin and of survival value are suspect. Friendship's certificates are not very satisfactory. Again, that outlook which values the collective above the individual necessarily disparages Friendship; it is a relation between men at their highest level of individuality. It withdraws men from collective "togetherness" as surely as solitude itself could do; and more dangerously, for it withdraws them by two's and three's. Some forms of democratic sentiment are naturally hostile to it because it is selective and an affair of the few. To say "These are my friends" implies "Those are not." For all these reasons if a man believes (as I do) that the old estimate of Friendship was the correct one, he can hardly write a chapter on it except as a rehabilitation.

This imposes on me at the outset a very tiresome bit of demolition. It has actually become necessary in our time to rebut the theory that every firm and serious friendship is really homosexual.

The dangerous word *really* is here important. To say that every Friendship is consciously and explicitly homosexual would be too obviously false; the wiseacres take refuge in the less palpable charge that it is *really*—unconsciously, cryptically, in some Pickwickian sense—homosexual. And this, though it cannot be proved, can never of course be refuted. The fact that no positive evidence of homosexuality can be discovered in the behaviour of two Friends does not disconcert the wiseacres at all: "That," they say gravely, "is just what we should expect." The very lack of evidence is thus treated as evidence; the absence of smoke proves that the fire is very carefully hidden. Yes—if it exists at all. But we must first prove its existence. Otherwise we are arguing like a man who should say "If there were an invisible cat in that chair, the chair would look empty; but the chair does look empty; therefore there is an invisible cat in it."

A belief in invisible cats cannot perhaps be logically disproved, but it tells us a good deal about those who hold it. Those who cannot conceive Friendship as a substantive love but only as a disguise or elaboration of Eros betray the fact that they have never had a Friend. The rest of us know that though we can have erotic love and friendship for the same person yet in some ways nothing is less like a Friendship than a love-affair. Lovers are always talking to one another about their love; Friends hardly ever about their Friendship. Lovers are normally face to face, absorbed in each other; Friends, side by side, absorbed in some common interest. Above all, Eros (while it lasts) is necessarily between two only. But two, far from being the necessary number for Friendship, is not even the best. And the reason for this is important.

Lamb says somewhere that if, of three friends (A, B, and C), A should die, then B loses not only A but "A's part in C," while C loses not only A but "A's part in B." In each of my friends there is something that only some other friend can fully bring out. By myself I am not large enough to call the whole man into activity; I want other lights than my own to show all his facets. Now that Charles is dead, I shall never again see Ronald's reaction to a specifically Caroline joke. Far from having more of Ronald, having him "to myself" now that Charles is away, I have less of Ronald. Hence true Friendship is the least jealous of loves. Two friends delight to be joined by a third, and three by a fourth, if only the newcomer is qualified to become a real friend. They can then say, as the blessed souls say in Dante, "Here comes one who will augment our loves." For in this love "to divide is not to take away." Of course the scarcity of kindred souls—not to mention practical considerations about the size of rooms and the audibility of voices—set limits to the enlargement of the circle; but within those limits we possess each friend not less but more as the number of those with whom we share him increases. In this, Friendship exhibits a glorious "nearness by resemblance" to Heaven itself where the very multitude of the blessed (which no man can number) increases the fruition which each has of God. For every soul, seeing Him in her own way, doubtless communicates that unique vision to all the rest. That, says an old author, is why the Seraphim in Isaiah's vision are crying "Holy, Holy, Holy" *to one another* (Isaiah VI, 3). The more we thus share the Heavenly Bread between us, the more we shall all have.

The homosexual theory therefore seems to me not even plausible. This is not to say that Friendship and abnormal Eros have never been combined. Certain cultures at certain periods seem to have tended to the contamination. In war-like societies it was, I think, especially likely to creep into the relation between the mature Brave and his young armour-bearer or squire. The absence of the women while you were on the war-path had no doubt something to do with it. In deciding, if we think we need or can decide, where it crept in and where it did not, we must surely be guided by the evidence (when there is any) and not by an *a priori* theory. Kisses, tears and embraces are not in themselves evidence of homosexuality. The implications would be, if nothing else, too comic. Hrothgar embracing Beowulf, Johnson embracing Boswell (a pretty flagrantly heterosexual couple) and all those hairy old toughs of centurions in Tacitus, clinging to one another and begging for last kisses when the legion was broken up . . . all pansies? If you can believe that you can believe anything. On a broad historical view it is, of course, not the demonstrative gestures of Friendship among our ancestors but the absence of such gestures in our own society that calls for some special explanation. We, not they, are out of step.

I have said that Friendship is the least biological of our loves. Both the individual and the community can survive without it. But there is something else, often confused with Friendship, which the community does need; something which, though not Friendship, is the matrix of Friendship.

In early communities the co-operation of the males as hunters or fighters was no less necessary than the begetting and rearing of children. A tribe where there was no taste for the one would die no less surely than a tribe where there was no taste for the other. Long before history began we men have got together apart from the women and done things. We had to. And to like doing what must be done is a characteristic that has survival value. We not only had to do the things, we had to talk about them. We had to plan the hunt and the battle. When they were over we had to hold a *post mortem* and draw conclusions for future use. We liked this even better. We ridiculed or punished the cowards and bunglers, we praised the star-performers. We revelled in technicalities. ("He might have known he'd never get near the brute, not with the wind that way" . . . "You see, I had a lighter arrowhead; that's what did it" . . . "What I always say is——" . . . "stuck him just like that, see? Just the way I'm holding this stick" . . .) In fact, we talked shop. We enjoyed one another's society greatly: we Braves, we hunters, all bound together by shared skill, shared dangers and hardships, esoteric jokes—

away from the women and children. As some wag has said, palaeolithic man may or may not have had a club on his shoulder but he certainly had a club of the other sort. It was probably part of his religion; like that sacred smoking-club where the savages in Melville's *Typee* were "famously snug" every evening of their lives.

What were the women doing meanwhile? How should I know? I am a man and never spied on the mysteries of the Bona Dea. They certainly often had rituals from which men were excluded. When, as sometimes happened, agriculture was in their hands, they must, like the men, have had common skills, toils and triumphs. Yet perhaps their world was never as emphatically feminine as that of their menfolk was masculine. The children were with them; perhaps the old men were there too. But I am only guessing. I can trace the pre-history of Friendship only in the male line.

This pleasure in co-operation, in talking shop, in the mutual respect and understanding of men who daily see one another tested, is biologically valuable. You may, if you like, regard it as a product of the "gregarious instinct." To me that seems a round-about way of getting at something which we all understand far better already than anyone has ever understood the word *instinct*— something which is going on at this moment in dozens of ward-rooms, bar-rooms, common-rooms, messes and golf-clubs. I prefer to call it Companionship—or Club-bableness.

This Companionship is, however, only the matrix of Friendship. It is often called Friendship, and many people when they speak of their "friends" mean only their companions. But it is not Friendship in the sense I give to the word. By saying this I do not at all intend to disparage the merely Clubbable relation. We do not disparage silver by distinguishing it from gold.

Friendship arises out of mere Companionship when two or more of the companions discover that they have in common some insight or interest or even taste which the others do not share and which, till that moment, each believed to be his own unique treasure (or burden). The typical expression of opening Friendship would be something like, "What? You too? I thought I was the only one." We can imagine that among those early hunters and warriors single individuals—one in a century? one in a thousand years?—saw what others did not; saw that the deer was beautiful as well as edible, that hunting was fun as well as necessary, dreamed that his gods might be not only powerful but holy. But as long as each of these percipient persons dies without finding a kindred soul, nothing (I suspect) will come of it; art or sport or spiritual religion will not be born. It is when two such persons discover one another, when, whether with immense difficulties and semi-articulate fumblings or with what would seem to us amazing and elliptical speed, they share their vision—it is then that Friendship is born. And instantly they stand together in an immense solitude.

Lovers seek for privacy. Friends find this solitude about them, this barrier between them and the herd, whether they want it or not. They would be glad to reduce it. The first two would be glad to find a third.

In our own time Friendship arises in the same way. For us of course the shared activity and therefore the companionship on which Friendship supervenes will not often be a bodily one like hunting or fighting. It may be a common religion, common studies, a common profession, even a common recreation. All who share it will be our companions; but one or two or three who share something more will be our Friends. In this kind of love, as Emerson said, *Do you love me?* means *Do you see the same truth?*—Or at least, "Do you *care about* the same truth?" The man who agrees with us that some question, little regarded by others, is of great importance can be our Friend. He need not agree with us about the answer.

Notice that Friendship thus repeats on a more individual and less socially necessary level the character of the Companionship which was its matrix. The Companionship was between people who were doing something together—hunting, studying, painting or what you will. The Friends will still be doing something together, but something more inward, less widely shared and less easily defined; still hunters, but of some immaterial quarry; still collaborating, but in some work the world does not, or not yet, take account of; still travelling companions, but on a different kind of journey. Hence we picture lovers face to face but Friends side by side; their eyes look ahead.

That is why those pathetic people who simply "want friends" can never make any. The very condition of having Friends is that we should want something else besides Friends. Where the truthful answer to the question *Do you see the same truth?* would be "I see nothing and I don't care about the truth; I only want a Friend," no Friendship can arise—though Affection of course may. There would be nothing for the Friendship to be *about;* and Friendship must be about something, even if it were only an enthusiasm for dominoes or white mice.

Those who have nothing can share nothing; those who are going nowhere can have no fellow-travellers.

When the two people who thus discover that they are on the same secret road are of different sexes, the friendship which arises between them will very easily pass—may pass in the first half-hour—into erotic love. Indeed, unless they are physically repulsive to each other or unless one or both already loves elsewhere, it is almost certain to do so sooner or later. And conversely, erotic love may lead to Friendship between the lovers. But this, so far from obliterating the distinction between the two loves, puts it in a clearer light. If one who was first, in the deep and full sense, your Friend, is then gradually or suddenly revealed as also your lover you will certainly not want to share the Beloved's erotic love with any third. But you will have no jealousy at all about sharing the Friendship. Nothing so enriches an erotic love as the discovery that the Beloved can deeply, truly and spontaneously enter into Friendship with the Friends you already had: to feel that not only are we two united by erotic love but we three or four or five are all travellers on the same quest, have all a common vision.

The co-existence of Friendship and Eros may also help some moderns to realise that Friendship is in reality a love, and even as great a love as Eros. Suppose you are fortunate enough to have "fallen in love with" and married your Friend. And now suppose it possible that you were offered the choice of two futures: "*Either* you two will cease to be lovers but remain forever joint seekers of the same God, the same beauty, the same truth, *or else,* losing all that, you will retain as long as you live the raptures and ardours, all the wonder and the wild desire of Eros. Choose which you please." Which should we choose? Which choice should we not regret after we had made it?

I have stressed the "unnecessary" character of Friendship, and this of course requires more justification than I have yet given it.

It could be argued that Friendships are of practical value to the Community. Every civilised religion began in a small group of friends. Mathematics effectively began when a few Greek friends got together to talk about numbers and lines and angles. What is now the Royal Society was originally a few gentlemen meeting in their spare time to discuss things which they (and not many others) had a fancy for. What we now call "the Romantic Movement" once *was* Mr. Wordsworth and Mr. Coleridge talking incessantly (at least Mr. Coleridge was) about a secret vision of their own. Communism, Tractarianism, Methodism, the movement against slavery, the Reformation, the Renaissance, might perhaps be said, without much exaggeration, to have begun in the same way.

There is something in this. But nearly every reader would probably think some of these movements good for society and some bad. The whole list, if accepted, would tend to show, at best, that Friendship is both a possible benefactor and a possible danger to the community. And even as a benefactor it would have, not so much survival value, as what we may call "civilisation-value"; would be something (in Aristotelian phrase) which helps the community not to live but to live well. Survival value and civilisation value coincide at some periods and in some circumstances, but not in all. What at any rate seems certain is that when Friendship bears fruit which the community can use it has to do so accidentally, as a by-product. Religions devised for a social purpose, like Roman emperor-worship or modern attempts to "sell" Christianity as a means of "saving civilisation," do not come to much. The little knots of Friends who turn their backs on the "World" are those who really transform it. Egyptian and Babylonian Mathematics were practical and social, pursued in the service of Agriculture and Magic. But the free Greek Mathematics, pursued by Friends as a leisure occupation, have mattered to us more.

Others again would say that Friendship is extremely useful, perhaps necessary for survival, to the individual. They could produce plenty of authority: "bare is back without brother behind it" and "there is a friend that sticketh closer than a brother." But when we speak thus we are using *friend* to mean "ally." In ordinary usage *friend* means, or should mean, more than that. A Friend will, to be sure, prove himself to be also an ally when alliance becomes necessary; will lend or give when we are in need, nurse us in sickness, stand up for us among our enemies, do what he can for our widows and orphans. But such good offices are not the stuff of Friendship. The occasions for them are almost interruptions. They are in one way relevant to it, in another not. Relevant, because you would be a false friend if you would not do them when the need arose; irrelevant, because the role of benefactor always remains accidental, even a little alien, to that of Friend. It is almost embarrassing. For Friendship is utterly free from Affection's need to be needed. We are sorry that any gift or loan or night-watching should have been necessary—and now, for heaven's sake, let us forget all about it and go back to the things we really want to do or talk of together. Even gratitude is no enrichment to this love. The stereotyped "Don't mention it" here expresses what we really feel. The mark of perfect Friendship is not that help will be given when the pinch comes (of course it will) but that, having been given, it makes no difference at all. It was a distraction, an anomaly. It was a horrible waste of the time, always too short, that we had together. Perhaps we had only a couple of hours in which to talk and, God bless us, twenty minutes of it has had to be devoted to *affairs!*

For of course we do not want to know our Friend's affairs at all. Friendship, unlike Eros, is uninquisitive. You become a man's Friend without knowing or caring whether he is married or single or how he earns his living. What have all these "unconcerning things, matters of fact" to do with the real question, *Do you see the same truth?* In a circle of true Friends each man is simply what he is: stands for nothing but himself. No one cares two-pence about anyone else's family, profession, class, income, race, or previous history. Of course you will get to know about most of these in the end. But casually. They will come out bit by bit, to furnish an illustration or an analogy, to serve as pegs for an anecdote; never for their own sake. That is the kingliness of Friendship. We meet like sovereign princes of independent states, abroad, on neutral ground, freed from our contexts. This love (essentially) ignores not only our physical bodies but that whole embodiment which consists of our family, job, past and connections. At home, besides being Peter or Jane, we also bear a general character; husband or wife, brother or sister, chief, colleague or subordinate. Not among our Friends. It is an affair of disentangled, or stripped, minds. Eros will have naked bodies; Friendship naked personalities.

Hence (if you will not misunderstand me) the exquisite arbitrariness and irresponsibility of this love. I have no duty to be anyone's Friend and no man in the world has a duty to be mine. No claims, no shadow of necessity. Friendship is unnecessary, like philosophy, like art, like the universe itself (for God did not need to create). It has no survival value; rather it is one of those things which give value to survival.

When I spoke of Friends as side by side or shoulder to shoulder I was pointing a necessary contrast between their posture and that of the lovers whom we picture face to face. Beyond that contrast I do not want the image pressed. The common quest or vision which unites Friends does not absorb them in such a way that they remain ignorant or oblivious of one another. On the contrary it is the very medium in which their mutual love and knowledge exist. One knows nobody so well as one's "fellow." Every step of the common journey tests his metal; and the tests are tests we fully understand because we are undergoing them ourselves. Hence, as he rings true time after time, our reliance, our respect and our admiration blossom into an Appreciative love of a singularly robust and well-informed kind. If, at the outset, we had attended more to him and less to the thing our Friendship is "about," we should not have come to know or love him so well. You will not find the warrior, the poet, the philosopher or the Christian by staring in his eyes as if he were your mistress: better fight beside him, read with him, argue with him, pray with him.

In a perfect Friendship this Appreciative love is, I

think, often so great and so firmly based that each member of the circle feels, in his secret heart, humbled before all the rest. Sometimes he wonders what he is doing there among his betters. He is lucky beyond desert to be in such company. Especially when the whole group is together, each bringing out all that is best, wisest, or funniest in all the others. Those are the golden sessions; when four or five of us after a hard day's walking have come to our inn; when our slippers are on, our feet spread out towards the blaze and our drinks at our elbows; when the whole world, and something beyond the world, opens itself to our minds as we talk; and no one has any claim on or any responsibility for another, but all are freemen and equals as if we had first met an hour ago, while at the same time an Affection mellowed by the years enfolds us. Life—natural life—has no better gift to give. Who could have deserved it?

From what has been said it will be clear that in most societies at most periods Friendships will be between men and men or between women and women. The sexes will have met one another in Affection and in Eros but not in this love. For they will seldom have had with each other the companionship in common activities which is the matrix of Friendship. Where men are educated and women not, where one sex works and the other is idle, or where they do totally different work, they will usually have nothing to be Friends about. But we can easily see that it is this lack, rather than anything in their natures, which excludes Friendship; for where they can be companions they can also become Friends. Hence in a profession (like my own) where men and women work side by side, or in the mission field, or among authors and artists, such Friendship is common. To be sure, what is offered as Friendship on one side may be mistaken for Eros on the other, with painful and embarrassing results. Or what begins as Friendship in both may become also Eros. But to say that something can be mistaken for, or turn into, something else is not to deny the difference between them. Rather it implies it; we should not otherwise speak of "turning into" or being "mistaken for."

In one respect our own society is unfortunate. A world where men and women never have common work or a common education can probably get along comfortably enough. In it men turn to each other, and only to each other, for Friendship, and they enjoy it very much. I hope the women enjoy their feminine Friends equally. Again, a world where all men and women had sufficient common ground for this relationship could also be comfortable. At present, however, we fall between two stools. The necessary common ground, the matrix, exists between the sexes in some groups but not in others. It is notably lacking in many residential suburbs. In a plutocratic neighbourhood where the men have spent their whole lives in acquiring money some at least of the women have used their leisure to develop an intellectual life—have become musical or literary. In such places the men appear among the women as barbarians among civilised people. In another neighbourhood you will find the situation reversed. Both sexes have, indeed, "been to school." But since then the men have had a much more serious education; they have become doctors, lawyers, clergymen, architects, engineers, or men of letters. The women are to them as children to adults. In neither neighbourhood is real Friendship between the sexes at all probable. But this, though an impoverishment, would be tolerable if it were admitted and accepted. The peculiar trouble of our own age is that men and women in this situation, haunted by rumours and glimpses of happier groups where no such chasm between the sexes exists, and bedevilled by the egalitarian idea that what is possible for some ought to be (and therefore is) possible to all, refuse to acquiesce in it. Hence, on the one hand, we get the wife as school-marm, the "cultivated" woman who is always trying to bring her husband "up to her level." She drags him to concerts and would like him to learn morris-dancing and invites "cultivated" people to the house. It often does surprisingly little harm. The middle-aged male has great powers of passive resistance and (if she but knew) of indulgence; "women will have their fads." Something much more painful happens when it is the men who are civilised and the women not, and when all the women, and many of the men too, simply refuse to recognise the fact.

When this happens we get a kind, polite, laborious and pitiful pretence. The women are "deemed" (as lawyers say) to be full members of the male circle. The fact—in itself not important—that they now smoke and drink like the men seems to simple-minded people a proof that they really are. No stag-parties are allowed. Wherever the men meet, the women must come too. The men have learned to live among ideas. They know what discussion, proof and illustration mean. A woman who has had merely school lessons and has abandoned soon after marriage whatever tinge of "culture" they gave her—whose reading is the Women's Magazines and whose general conversation is almost wholly narrative— cannot really enter such a circle. She can be locally and physically present with it in the same room. What of that? If the men are ruthless, she sits bored and silent through a conversation which means nothing to her. If they are better bred, of course, they try to bring her in. Things are explained to her: people try to sublimate her irrelevant and blundering observations into some kind of sense. But the efforts soon fail and, for manners' sake, what might have been a real discussion is deliberately diluted and peters out in gossip, anecdotes, and jokes. Her presence has thus destroyed the very thing she was brought to share. She can never really enter the circle because the circle ceases to be itself when she enters it— as the horizon ceases to be the horizon when you get there. By learning to drink and smoke and perhaps to tell *risqué* stories, she has not, for this purpose, drawn an inch nearer to the men than her grandmother. But her grandmother was far happier and more realistic. She was at home talking real women's talk to other women and perhaps doing so with great charm, sense and even wit. She herself might be able to do the same. She may be quite as clever as the men whose evening she has spoiled, or cleverer. But she is not really interested in the same things, nor mistress of the same methods. (We all appear as dunces when feigning an interest in things we care nothing about.)

The presence of such women, thousands strong, helps to account for the modern disparagement of Friendship. They are often completely victorious. They banish male companionship, and therefore male Friendship, from whole neighbourhoods. In the only world they know, an endless prattling "Jolly" replaces the intercourse of minds. All the men they meet talk like women while women are present.

This victory over Friendship is often unconscious. There is, however, a more militant type of woman who plans it. I have heard one say "Never let two men sit together or they'll get talking about some *subject* and then there'll be no fun." Her point could not have been more accurately made. Talk, by all means; the more of it the better; unceasing cascades of the human voice; but not, please, a subject. The talk must not be about anything.

This gay lady—this lively, accomplished, "charming," unendurable bore—was seeking only each evening's amusement, making the meeting "go." But the conscious war against Friendship may be fought on a deeper level. There are women who regard it with hatred, envy and fear as the enemy of Eros and, perhaps even more, of Affection. A woman of that sort has a hundred arts to break up her husband's Friendships. She will quarrel with his Friends herself or, better still, with their wives. She will sneer, obstruct and lie. She does not realise that the husband whom she succeeds in isolating from his own kind will not be very well worth having; she has emasculated him. She will grow to be ashamed of him herself. Nor does she remember how much of his life lies in places where she cannot watch him. New Friendships will break out, but this time they will be secret. Lucky for her, and lucky beyond her deserts, if there are not soon other secrets as well.

All these, of course, are silly women. The sensible women who, if they wanted, would certainly be able to qualify themselves for the world of discussion and ideas, are precisely those who, if they are not qualified, never try to enter it or to destroy it. They have other fish to fry. At a mixed party they gravitate to one end of the room and talk women's talk to one another. They don't want us, for this sort of purpose, any more than we want them. It is only the riff-raff of each sex that wants to be incessantly hanging on the other. Live and let live. They laugh at us a good deal. That is just as it should be. Where the sexes, having no real shared activities, can meet only in Affection and Eros—cannot be Friends— it is healthy that each should have a lively sense of the other's absurdity. Indeed it is always healthy. No one ever really appreciated the other sex—just as no one really appreciates children or animals—without at times feeling them to be funny. For both sexes are. Humanity is tragi-comical; but the division into sexes enables each to see in the other the joke that often escapes it in itself—and the pathos too.

I gave warning that this chapter would be largely a rehabilitation. The preceding pages have, I hope, made clear why to me at least it seems no wonder if our ancestors regarded Friendship as something that raised us almost above humanity. This love, free from instinct, free from all duties but those which love has freely assumed, almost wholly free from jealousy, and free without qualification from the need to be needed, is eminently spiritual. It is the sort of love one can imagine between angels. Have we here found a natural love which is Love itself?

Before we rush to any such conclusion let us beware of the ambiguity in the word *spiritual*. There are many New Testament contexts in which it means "pertaining to the (Holy) Spirit," and in such contexts the spiritual is, by definition, good. But when *spiritual* is used simply as the opposite of corporeal, or instinctive, or animal, this is not so. There is spiritual evil as well as spiritual good. There are unholy, as well as holy, angels. The worst sins of men are spiritual. We must not think that in finding Friendship to be *spiritual* we have found it to be in itself holy or inerrant. Three significant facts remain to be taken into account.

The first, already mentioned, is the distrust which Authorities tend to have of close Friendships among their subjects. It may be unjustified; or there may be some basis for it.

Secondly, there is the attitude of the majority towards all circles of close Friends. Every name they give such a circle is more or less derogatory. It is at best a "set"; lucky if not a *coterie*, a "gang," a "little senate," or a "mutual admiration society." Those who in their own lives know only Affection, Companionship and Eros, suspect Friends to be "stuck-up prigs who think themselves too good for us." Of course this is the voice of Envy. But Envy always brings the truest charge, or the charge nearest to the truth, that she can think up; it hurts more. This charge, therefore, will have to be considered.

Finally, we must notice that Friendship is very rarely the image under which Scripture represents the love between God and Man. It is not entirely neglected; but far more often, seeking a symbol for the highest love of all, Scripture ignores this seemingly almost angelic relation and plunges into the depth of what is most natural and instinctive. Affection is taken as the image when God is represented as our Father; Eros, when Christ is represented as the Bridegroom of the Church.

Let us begin with the suspicions of those in Authority. I think there is a ground for them and that a consideration of this ground brings something important to light. Friendship, I have said, is born at the moment when one man says to another "What! You too? I thought that no one but myself . . ." But the common taste or vision or point of view which is thus discovered need not always be a nice one. From such a moment art, or philosophy, or an advance in religion or morals might well take their rise; but why not also torture, cannibalism, or human sacrifice? Surely most of us have experienced the ambivalent nature of such moments in our own youth? It was wonderful when we first met someone who cared for our favourite poet. What we had hardly understood before now took clear shape. What we had been half ashamed of we now freely acknowledged. But it was no less delightful when we first met someone who shared with us a secret evil. This too became far more palpable and explicit; of this too, we ceased to be ashamed. Even now, at whatever age, we all know the perilous charm of a shared hatred or grievance. (It is difficult not to hail as a Friend the only other man in College who really sees the faults of the Sub-Warden.)

Alone among unsympathetic companions, I hold certain views and standards timidly, half ashamed to avow them and half doubtful if they can after all be right. Put me back among my Friends and in half an hour—in ten minutes—these same views and standards become once more indisputable. The opinion of this little circle, while I am in it, outweighs that of a thousand outsiders: as Friendship strengthens, it will do this even when my Friends are far away. For we all wish to be judged by our peers, by the men "after our own heart." Only they really know our mind and only they judge it by standards we fully acknowledge. Theirs is the praise we really covet and the blame we really dread. The little pockets of early Christians survived because they cared exclusively for the love of "the brethren" and stopped their ears to the opinion of the Pagan society all round them. But a circle of criminals, cranks, or perverts survives in just the same way; by becoming deaf to the opinion of the outer world, by discounting it as the chatter of outsiders who "don't understand," of the "conventional," "the bourgeois," the "Establishment," of prigs, prudes and humbugs.

It is therefore easy to see why Authority frowns on Friendship. Every real Friendship is a sort of secession, even a rebellion. It may be a rebellion of serious thinkers against accepted clap-trap or of faddists against accepted good sense; of real artists against popular ugliness or of charlatans against civilised taste; of good men against the badness of society or of bad men against its goodness. Whichever it is, it will be unwelcome to Top People. In each knot of Friends there is a sectional "public opinion" which fortifies its members against the public opinion of the community in general. Each therefore is a pocket of potential resistance. Men who have real Friends are less easy to manage or "get at"; harder for good Authorities to correct or for bad Authorities to corrupt. Hence if our masters, by force or by propaganda about "Togetherness" or by unobtrusively making privacy and unplanned leisure impossible, ever succeed in producing a world where all are Companions and none are Friends, they will have removed certain dangers, and will also have taken from us what is almost our strongest safeguard against complete servitude.

But the dangers are perfectly real. Friendship (as the ancients saw) can be a school of virtue; but also (as they did not see) a school of vice. It is ambivalent. It makes good men better and bad men worse. It would be a waste of time to elaborate the point. What concerns us is not to expatiate on the badness of bad Friendships but to become aware of the possible danger in good ones. This love, like the other natural loves, has its congenital liability to a particular disease.

It will be obvious that the element of secession, of indifference or deafness (at least on some matters) to the voices of the outer world, is common to all Friendships, whether good, bad, or merely innocuous. Even if the common ground of the Friendship is nothing more momentous than stamp-collecting, the circle rightly and inevitably ignores the views of the millions who think it a silly occupation and of the thousands who have merely dabbled in it. The founders of meteorology rightly and inevitably ignored the views of the millions who still attributed storms to witchcraft. There is no offence in this. As I know that I should be an Outsider to a circle of golfers, mathematicians, or motorists, so I claim the equal right of regarding them as Outsiders to mine. People who bore one another should meet seldom; people who interest one another, often.

The danger is that this partial indifference or deafness to outside opinion, justified and necessary though it is, may lead to a wholesale indifference or deafness. The most spectacular instances of this can be seen not in a circle of Friends but in a Theocratic or aristocratic class. We know what the Priests in Our Lord's time thought of the common people. The Knights in Froissart's chronicles had neither sympathy nor mercy for the "outsiders," the churls or peasantry. But this deplorable indifference was very closely intertwined with a good quality. They really had, among themselves, a very high standard of valour, generosity, courtesy and honour. This standard the cautious, close-fisted churl would have thought merely silly. The Knights, in maintaining it, were, and had to be, wholly indifferent to his views.

They "didn't give a damn" what he thought. If they had, our own standard today would be the poorer and the coarser for it. But the habit of "not giving a damn" grows on a class. To discount the voice of the peasant where it really ought to be discounted makes it easier to discount his voice when he cries for justice or mercy. The partial deafness which is noble and necessary encourages the wholesale deafness which is arrogant and inhuman.

A circle of Friends cannot of course oppress the outer world as a powerful social class can. But it is subject, on its own scale, to the same danger. It can come to treat as "outsiders" in a general (and derogatory) sense those who were quite properly outsiders for a particular purpose. Thus, like an aristocracy, it can create around it a vacuum across which no voice will carry. The literary or artistic circle which began by discounting, perhaps rightly, the plain man's ideas about literature or art may come to discount equally his idea that they should pay their bills, cut their nails and behave civilly. Whatever faults the circle has—and no circle is without them— thus become incurable. But that is not all. The partial and defensible deafness was based on some kind of superiority—even if it were only a superior knowledge about stamps. The sense of superiority will then get itself attached to the total deafness. The group will disdain as well as ignore those outside it. It will, in effect, have turned itself into something very like a class. A *coterie* is a self-appointed aristocracy.

I said above that in a good Friendship each member often feels humility towards the rest. He sees that they are splendid and counts himself lucky to be among them. But unfortunately the *they* and *them* are also, from another point of view *we* and *us*. Thus the transition from individual humility to corporate pride is very easy.

I am not thinking of what we should call a social or snobbish pride: a delight in knowing, and being known to know, distinguished people. That is quite a different thing. The snob wishes to attach himself to some group because it is already regarded as an *élite;* friends are in danger of coming to regard themselves as an *élite* because they are already attached. We seek men after our own heart for their own sake and are then alarmingly or delightfully surprised by the feeling that we have become an aristocracy. Not that we'd call it that. Every reader who has known Friendship will probably feel inclined to deny with some heat that his own circle was ever guilty of such an absurdity. I feel the same. But in such matters it is best not to begin with ourselves. However it may be with us, I think we have all recognised some such tendency in those other circles to which we are the Outsiders.

I was once at some kind of conference where two clergymen, obviously close friends, began talking about "uncreated energies" other than God. I asked how there could be any uncreated things except God if the Creed was right in calling Him the "maker of all things visible and invisible." Their reply was to glance at one another and laugh. I had no objection to their laughter, but I wanted an answer in words as well. It was not at all a sneering or unpleasant laugh. It expressed very much what Americans would express by saying "Isn't he cute?" It was like the laughter of jolly grown-ups when an *enfant terrible* asks the sort of question that is never asked. You can hardly imagine how inoffensively it was done, nor how clearly it conveyed the impression that they were fully aware of living habitually on a higher plane than the rest of us, of coming among us as Knights among churls or as grown-ups among children. Very possibly they had an answer to my question and knew that I was too ignorant to follow it. If they had said in so many words "I'm afraid it would take too long to explain," I would not be attributing to them the pride of Friendship. The glance and the laugh are the real point—the audible and visible embodiment of a corporate superiority taken for granted and unconcealed. The almost complete inoffensiveness, the absence of any apparent wish to wound or exult (they were very nice young men) really underline the Olympian attitude. Here was a sense of superiority so secure that it could afford to be tolerant, urbane, unemphatic.

This sense of corporate superiority is not always Olympian; that is, tranquil and tolerant. It may be Titanic; restive, militant and embittered. Another time, when I had been addressing an undergraduate society and some discussion (very properly) followed my paper, a young man with an expression as tense as that of a rodent so dealt with me that I had to say, "Look, sir. Twice in the last five minutes you have as good as called me a liar. If you cannot discuss a question of criticism without that kind of thing I must leave." I expected he would do one of two things; lose his temper and redouble his insults, or else blush and apologise. The startling thing is that he did neither. No new perturbation was added to the habitual *malaise* of his expression. He did not repeat the Lie Direct; but apart from that he went on just as before. One had come up against an iron curtain. He was forearmed against the risk of any strictly personal relation, either friendly or hostile, with such as me. Behind this, almost certainly, there lies a circle of the Titanic sort—self-dubbed Knights Templars perpetually in arms to defend a critical Baphomet. We—who are *they* to them—do not exist as persons at all. We are specimens; specimens of various Age Groups, Types, Climates of Opinion, or Interests, to be exterminated. Deprived of one weapon, they cooly take up another. They are not, in the ordinary human sense, meeting us at all; they are merely doing a job of work—spraying (I have heard one use that image) insecticide.

My two nice young clergymen and my not so nice Rodent were on a high intellectual level. So were that famous set who in Edwardian times reached the sublime fatuity of calling themselves "the Souls." But the same feeling of corporate superiority can possess a group of much more commonplace friends. It will then be flaunted in a cruder way. We have all seen this done by the "old hands" at school talking in the presence of a new boy, or two Regulars in the Army talking before a "Temporary"; sometimes by very loud and vulgar friends to impress mere strangers in a bar or a railway carriage. Such people talk very intimately and esoterically in order to be overheard. Everyone who is not in the circle must be shown that he is not in it. Indeed the Friendship may be "about" almost nothing except the fact that it excludes. In speaking to an Outsider each member of it delights to mention the others by their Christian names or nicknames; not although, but because, the Outsider won't know who he means. A man I once knew was even subtler. He simply referred to his friends as if we all knew, certainly ought to know, who they were. "As Richard Button once said to me . . . ," he would begin. We were all very young. We never dared to admit that we hadn't heard of Richard Button. It seemed so obvious that to everyone who was anyone he must be a household word; "not to know him argued ourselves unknown." Only much later did we come to realise that no one else had heard of him either. (Indeed I now have a suspicion that some of these Richard Buttons, Hezekiah Cromwells, and Eleanor Forsyths had no more existence than Mrs. Harris. But for a year or so we were completely overawed.)

We can thus detect the pride of Friendship—whether Olympian, Titanic, or merely vulgar—in many circles of Friends. It would be rash to assume that our own is safe from its danger; for of course it is in our own that we should be slowest to recognise it. The danger of such pride is indeed almost inseparable from Friendly love. Friendship must exclude. From the innocent and necessary act of excluding to the spirit of exclusiveness is an easy step; and thence to the degrading pleasure of exclusiveness. If that is once admitted the downward slope will grow rapidly steeper. We may never perhaps become Titans or plain cads; we might—which is in some ways worse—become "Souls." The common vision which first brought us together may fade quite away. We shall be a *coterie* that exists for the sake of being a *coterie;* a little self-elected (and therefore absurd) aristocracy, basking in the moonshine of our collective self-approval.

Sometimes a circle in this condition begins to dabble in the world of practice. Judiciously enlarging itself to admit recruits whose share in the original common interest is negligible but who are felt to be (in some undefined sense) "sound men," it becomes a power in the land. Membership of it comes to have a sort of political importance, though the politics involved may be only those of a regiment, a college, or a cathedral close. The manipulation of committees, the capture of jobs (for sound men) and the united front against the Have-nots now become its principal occupation, and those who once met to talk about God or poetry now meet to talk about lectureships or livings. Notice the justice of their doom. "Dust thou art and unto dust shalt thou return," said God to Adam. In a circle which has thus dwindled into a coven of wanglers Friendship has sunk back again into the mere practical Companionship which was its matrix. They are now the same sort of body as the primitive horde of hunters. Hunters, indeed, is precisely what they are; and not the kind of hunters I most respect.

The mass of the people, who are never quite right, are never quite wrong. They are hopelessly mistaken in their belief that every knot of friends came into existence for the sake of the pleasures of conceit and superiority. They are, I trust, mistaken in their belief that every Friendship actually indulges in these pleasures. But they would seem to be right in diagnosing pride as the danger to which Friendships are naturally liable. Just because this is the most spiritual of loves the danger which besets it is spiritual too. Friendship is even, if you like, angelic. But man needs to be triply protected by humility if he is to eat the bread of angels without risk.

Perhaps we may now hazard a guess why Scripture uses Friendship so rarely as an image of the highest love. It is already, in actual fact, too spiritual to be a good symbol of Spiritual things. The highest does not stand without the lowest. God can safely represent Himself to us as Father and Husband because only a lunatic would think that He is physically our sire or that His marriage with the Church is other than mystical. But if Friendship were used for this purpose we might mistake the symbol for the thing symbolised. The danger inherent in it would be aggravated. We might be further encouraged to mistake that nearness (by resemblance) to the heavenly life which Friendship certainly displays for a nearness of approach.

Friendship, then, like the other natural loves, is unable to save itself. In reality, because it is spiritual and therefore faces a subtler enemy, it must, even more wholeheartedly than they, invoke the divine protection if it hopes to remain sweet. For consider how narrow its true path is. It must not become what the people call a "mutual admiration society"; yet if it is not full of mutual admiration, of Appreciative love, it is not Friendship at all. For unless our lives are to be miserably impoverished it must be for us in our Friendships as it was for Christiana and her party in *The Pilgrim's Progress:*

> *They seemed to be a terror one to the other, for that they could not see that glory each one on herself which they could see in each other. Now therefore they began to esteem each other better than themselves. For you are fairer than I am, said one; and you are more comely than I am, said another.*

There is in the long run only one way in which we can taste this illustrious experience with safety. And Bunyan has indicated it in the same passage. It was in the House of the Interpreter, after they had been bathed, sealed and freshly clothed in "White Raiment" that the women saw one another in this light. If we remember the bathing, sealing and robing, we shall be safe. And the higher the common ground of the Friendship is, the more necessary the remembrance. In an explicitly religious Friendship, above all, to forget it would be fatal.

For then it will seem to us that we—we four or five—have chosen one another, the insight of each finding the intrinsic beauty of the rest, like to like, a voluntary nobility; that we have ascended above the rest of mankind by our native powers. The other loves do not invite the same illusion. Affection obviously requires kinships or at least proximities which never depended on our own choice. And as for Eros, half the love songs and half the love poems in the world will tell you that the Beloved is your fate or destiny, no more your choice than a thunderbolt, for "it is not in our power to love or hate." Cupid's archery, genes—anything but ourselves. But in Friendship, being free of all that, we think we have chosen our peers. In reality, a few years' difference in the dates of our births, a few more miles between certain houses, the choice of one university instead of another, posting to different regiments, the accident of a topic being raised or not raised at a first meeting—any of these chances might have kept us apart. But, for a Christian, there are, strictly speaking, no chances. A secret Master of the Ceremonies has been at work. Christ, who said to the disciples "Ye have not chosen me, but I have chosen you," can truly say to every group of Christian friends "You have not chosen one another but I have chosen you for one another." The Friendship is not a reward for our discrimination and good taste in finding one another out. It is the instrument by which God reveals to each the beauties of all the others. They are no greater than the beauties of a thousand other men;

by Friendship God opens our eyes to them. They are, like all beauties, derived from Him, and then, in a good Friendship, increased by Him through the Friendship itself, so that it is His instrument for creating as well as for revealing. At this feast it is He who has spread the board and it is He who has chosen the guests. It is He, we may dare to hope, who sometimes does, and always should, preside. Let us not reckon without our Host.

Not that we must always partake of it solemnly. "God who made good laughter" forbid. It is one of the difficult and delightful subtleties of life that we must deeply acknowledge certain things to be serious and yet retain the power and will to treat them often as lightly as a game. But there will be a time for saying more about this in the next chapter. For the moment I will only quote Dunbar's beautifully balanced advice:

> *Man, please thy Maker, and be merry,*
> *And give not for this world a cherry.*

EROS

By Eros I mean of course that state which we call "being in love"; or, if you prefer, that kind of love which lovers are "in." Some readers may have been surprised when, in an earlier chapter, I described Affection as the love in which our experience seems to come closest to that of the animals. Surely, it might be asked, our sexual functions bring us equally close? This is quite true as regards human sexuality in general. But I am not going to be concerned with human sexuality simply as such. Sexuality makes part of our subject only when it becomes an ingredient in the complex state of "being in love." That sexual experience can occur without Eros, without being "in love," and that Eros includes other things besides sexual activity, I take for granted. If you prefer to put it that way, I am inquiring not into the sexuality which is common to us and the beasts or even common to all men but into one uniquely human variation of it which develops within "love"—what I call Eros. The carnal or animally sexual element within Eros, I intend (following an old usage) to call Venus. And I mean by Venus what is sexual not in some cryptic or rarefied sense—such as a depth-psychologist might explore—but in a perfectly obvious sense; what is known to be sexual by those who experience it; what could be proved to be sexual by the simplest observations.

Sexuality may operate without Eros or as part of Eros. Let me hasten to add that I make the distinction simply in order to limit our inquiry and without any moral implications. I am not at all subscribing to the popular idea that it is the absence or presence of Eros which makes the sexual act "impure" or "pure," degraded or fine, unlawful or lawful. If all who lay together without being in the state of Eros were abominable, we all come of tainted stock. The times and places in which marriage depends on Eros are in a small minority. Most of our ancestors were married off in early youth to partners chosen by their parents on grounds that had nothing to do with Eros. They went to the act with no other "fuel," so to speak, than plain animal desire. And they did right; honest Christian husbands and wives, obeying their fathers and mothers, discharging to one another their "marriage debt," and bringing up families in the fear of the Lord. Conversely, this act, done under the influence of a soaring and iridescent Eros which reduces the role of the senses to a minor consideration, may yet be plain adultery, may involve breaking a wife's heart, deceiving a husband, betraying a friend, polluting hospitality and deserting your children. It has not pleased God that the distinction between a sin and a duty should turn on fine feelings. This act, like any other, is justified (or not) by far more prosaic and definable criteria; by the keeping or breaking of promises, by justice or injustice, by charity or selfishness, by obedience or disobedience. My treatment rules out mere sexuality—sexuality without Eros—on grounds that have nothing to do with morals; because it is irrelevant to our purpose.

To the evolutionist Eros (the human variation) will be something that grows out of Venus, a late complication and development of the immemorial biological impulse. We must not assume, however, that this is necessarily what happens within the consciousness of the individual. There may be those who have first felt mere sexual appetite for a woman and then gone on at a later stage to "fall in love with her." But I doubt if this is at all common. Very often what comes first is simply a delighted pre-occupation with the Beloved—a general, unspecified pre-occupation with her in her totality. A man in this state really hasn't leisure to think of sex. He is too busy thinking of a person. The fact that she is a woman is far less important than the fact that she is herself. He is full of desire, but the desire may not be sexually toned. If you asked him what he wanted, the true reply would often be, "To go on thinking of her." He is love's contemplative. And when at a later stage the explicitly sexual element awakes, he will not feel (unless scientific theories are influencing him) that this had all along been the root of the whole matter. He is more likely to feel that the incoming tide of Eros, having demolished many sandcastles and made islands of many rocks, has now at last with a triumphant seventh wave flooded this part of his nature also—the little pool of ordinary sexuality which was there on his beach before the tide came in. Eros enters him like an invader, taking over and reorganising, one by one, the institutions of a conquered country. It may have taken over many others before it reaches the sex in him; and it will reorganise that too.

No one has indicated the nature of that reorganisation more briefly and accurately than George Orwell, who disliked it and preferred sexuality in its native condition, uncontaminated by Eros. In *Nineteen Eighty-Four* his dreadful hero (how much less human than the four-footed heroes of his excellent *Animal Farm!*), before towsing the heroine, demands a reassurance, "You like doing this?" he asks, "I don't mean simply me; I mean the thing in itself." He is not satisfied till he gets the answer, "I adore it." This little dialogue defines the reorganisation. Sexual desire, without Eros, wants *it*, the *thing in itself*; Eros wants the Beloved.

The *thing* is a sensory pleasure; that is, an event occuring within one's own body. We use a most unfortunate idiom when we say, of a lustful man prowling the streets, that he "wants a woman." Strictly speaking, a woman is just what he does not want. He wants a pleasure for which a woman happens to be the necessary piece of apparatus. How much he cares about the woman as such may be gauged by his attitude to her five minutes after fruition (one does not keep the carton after one has smoked the cigarettes). Now Eros makes a man really want, not a woman, but one particular woman. In some mysterious but quite indisputable fashion the lover desires the Beloved herself, not the pleasure she can give. No lover in the world ever sought the embraces of the woman he loved as the result of a calculation, however unconscious, that they would be more pleasurable than those of any other woman. If he raised the question he would, no doubt, expect that this would be so. But to raise it would be to step outside the world of Eros altogether. The only man I know of who ever did raise it was Lucretius, and he was certainly not in love when he did. It is interesting to note his answer. That austere voluptuary gave it as his opinion that love actually impairs sexual pleasure. The emotion was a distraction. It spoiled the cool and critical receptivity of his palate. (A great poet; but "Lord, what beastly fellows these Romans were!")

The reader will notice that Eros thus wonderfully transforms what is *par excellence* a Need-pleasure into the most Appreciative of all pleasures. It is the nature of a Need-pleasure to show us the object solely in relation to our need, even our momentary need. But in Eros, a Need, at its most intense, sees the object most intensely as a thing admirable in herself, important far beyond her relation to the lover's need.

If we had not all experienced this, if we were mere logicians, we might boggle at the conception of desiring a human being, as distinct from desiring any pleasure, comfort, or service that human being can give. And it is certainly hard to explain. Lovers themselves are trying to express part of it (not much) when they say they would like to "eat" one another. Milton has expressed more when he fancies angelic creatures with bodies made of light who can achieve total interpenetration instead of our mere embraces. Charles Williams has said something of it in the words, "Love you? I *am* you."

Without Eros sexual desire, like every other desire, is a fact about ourselves. Within Eros it is rather about the Beloved. It becomes almost a mode of perception, entirely a mode of expression. It feels objective; something outside us, in the real world. That is why Eros, though the king of pleasures, always (at his height) has the air of regarding pleasure as a by-product. To think about it would plunge us back in ourselves, in our own nervous system. It would kill Eros, as you can "kill" the finest mountain prospect by locating it all in your own retina and optic nerves. Anyway, whose pleasure? For one of the first things Eros does is to obliterate the distinction between giving and receiving.

Hitherto I have been trying merely to describe, not to evaluate. But certain moral questions now inevitably arise, and I must not conceal my own view of them. It is submitted rather than asserted, and of course open to correction by better men, better lovers and better Christians.

It has been widely held in the past, and is perhaps held by many unsophisticated people to-day, that the spiritual danger of Eros arises almost entirely from the carnal element within it; that Eros is "noblest" or "purest" when Venus is reduced to the minimum. The older moral theologians certainly seem to have thought that the danger we chiefly had to guard against in marriage was that of a soul-destroying surrender to the senses. It will be noticed, however, that this is not the Scriptural approach. St. Paul, dissuading his converts from marriage, says nothing about that side of the matter except to discourage prolonged abstinence from Venus (1 *Cor.* VII, 5). What he fears is pre-occupation, the need of constantly "pleasing"—that is, considering—one's partner, the multiple distractions of domesticity. It is marriage itself, not the marriage bed, that will be likely to hinder us from waiting uninterruptedly on God. And surely St. Paul is right? If I may trust my own experience, it is (within marriage as without) the practical and prudential cares of this world, and even the smallest and most prosaic of those cares, that are the great distraction. The gnat-like cloud of petty anxieties and decisions about the conduct of the next hour have interfered with my prayers more often than any passion or appetite whatever. The great, permanent temptation of marriage is not to sensuality but (quite bluntly) to avarice. With all proper respect to the medieval guides, I cannot help remembering that they were all celibates, and probably did not know what Eros does to our sexuality; how, far from aggravating, he reduces the nagging and addictive character of mere appetite. And that not simply by satisfying it. Eros, without diminishing desire, makes abstinence easier. He tends, no doubt, to a pre-occupation with the Beloved which can indeed be an obstacle to the spiritual life; but not chiefly a sensual pre-occupation.

The real spiritual danger in Eros as a whole lies, I believe, elsewhere. I will return to the point. For the moment, I want to speak of the danger which at present, in my opinion, especially haunts the act of love. This is a subject on which I disagree, not with the human race (far from it), but with many of its gravest spokesmen. I believe we are all being encouraged to take Venus too seriously; at any rate, with a wrong kind of seriousness. All my life a ludicrous and portentous solemnisation of sex has been going on.

One author tells us that Venus should recur through the married life in "a solemn, sacramental rhythm." A young man to whom I had described as "pornographic" a novel that he much admired, replied with genuine bewilderment, "Pornographic? But how can it be? It treats the whole thing so seriously"—as if a long face were a sort of moral disinfectant. Our friends who harbour

Dark Gods, the "pillar of blood" school, attempt seriously to restore something like the Phallic religion. Our advertisements, at their sexiest, paint the whole business in terms of the rapt, the intense, the swoony-devout; seldom a hint of gaiety. And the psychologists have so bedevilled us with the infinite importance of complete sexual adjustment and the all but impossibility of achieving it, that I could believe some young couples now go to it with the complete works of Freud, Kraft-Ebbing, Havelock Ellis and Dr. Stopes spread out on bed-tables all round them. Cheery old Ovid, who never either ignored a mole-hill or made a mountain of it, would be more to the point. We have reached the stage at which nothing is more needed than a roar of old-fashioned laughter.

But, it will be replied, the thing *is* serious. Yes; quadruply so. First, theologically, because this is the body's share in marriage which, by God's choice, is the mystical image of the union between God and Man. Secondly, as what I will venture to call a sub-Christian, or Pagan or natural sacrament, our human participation in, and exposition of, the natural forces of life and fertility— the marriage of Sky-Father and Earth-Mother. Thirdly, on the moral level, in view of the obligations involved and the incalculable momentousness of being a parent and ancestor. Finally it has (sometimes, not always) a great emotional seriousness in the minds of the participants.

But eating is also serious; theologically, as the vehicle of the Blessed Sacrament; ethically in view of our duty to feed the hungry; socially, because the table is from time immemorial the place for talk; medically, as all dyspeptics know. Yet we do not bring bluebooks to dinner nor behave there as if we were in church. And it is *gourmets,* not saints, who come nearest to doing so. Animals are always serious about food.

We must not be totally serious about Venus. Indeed we can't be totally serious without doing violence to our humanity. It is not for nothing that every language and literature in the world is full of jokes about sex. Many of them may be dull or disgusting and nearly all of them are old. But we must insist that they embody an attitude to Venus which in the long run endangers the Christian life far less than a reverential gravity. We must not attempt to find an absolute in the flesh. Banish play and laughter from the bed of love and you may let in a false goddess. She will be even falser than the Aphrodite of the Greeks; for they, even while they worshipped her, knew that she was "laughter-loving." The mass of the people are perfectly right in their conviction that Venus is a partly comic spirit. We are under no obligation at all to sing all our love-duets in the throbbing, world-without-end, heart-breaking manner of Tristan and Isolde; let us often sing like Papageno and Papagena instead.

Venus herself will have a terrible revenge if we take her (occasional) seriousness at its face value. And that in two ways. One is most comically—though with no comic intention—illustrated by Sir Thomas Browne when he says that her service is "the foolishest act a wise man commits in all his life, nor is there anything that will more deject his cool'd imagination, when he shall consider what an odd and unworthy piece of folly he hath committed." But if he had gone about that act with less solemnity in the first place he would not have suffered this "dejection." If his imagination had not been misled, its cooling would have brought no such revulsion. But Venus has another and worse revenge.

She herself is a mocking, mischievous spirit, far more elf than deity, and makes game of us. When all external circumstances are fittest for her service she will leave one or both the lovers totally indisposed for it. When every overt act is impossible and even glances cannot be exchanged—in trains, in shops, and at interminable parties—she will assail them with all her force. An hour later, when time and place agree, she will have mysteriously withdrawn; perhaps from only one of them. What a pother this must raise—what resentments, self-pities, suspicions, wounded vanities and all the current chatter about "frustration"—in those who have deified her! But sensible lovers laugh. It is all part of the game; a game of catch-as-catch-can, and the escapes and tumbles and head-on collisions are to be treated as a romp.

For I can hardly help regarding it as one of God's jokes that a passion so soaring, so apparently transcendent, as Eros, should thus be linked in incongruous symbiosis with a bodily appetite which, like any other appetite, tactlessly reveals its connections with such mundane factors as weather, health, diet, circulation, and digestion. In Eros at times we seem to be flying; Venus gives us the sudden twitch that reminds us we are really captive balloons. It is a continual demonstration of the truth that we are composite creatures, rational animals, akin on one side to the angels, on the other to tom-cats. It is a bad thing not to be able to take a joke. Worse, not to take a divine joke; made, I grant you, at our expense, but also (who doubts it?) for our endless benefit.

Man has held three views of his body. First there is

that of those ascetic Pagans who called it the prison or the "tomb" of the soul, and of Christians like Fisher to whom it was a "sack of dung," food for worms, filthy, shameful, a source of nothing but temptation to bad men and humiliation to good ones. Then there are the Neo-Pagans (they seldom know Greek), the nudists and the sufferers from Dark Gods, to whom the body is glorious. But thirdly we have the view which St. Francis expressed by calling his body "Brother Ass." All three may be— I am not sure—defensible; but give me St. Francis for my money.

Ass is exquisitely right because no one in his senses can either revere or hate a donkey. It is a useful, sturdy, lazy, obstinate, patient, lovable and infuriating beast; deserving now the stick and now a carrot; both pathetically and absurdly beautiful. So the body. There's no living with it till we recognise that one of its functions in our lives is to play the part of buffoon. Until some theory has sophisticated them, every man, woman and child in the world knows this. The fact that we have bodies is the oldest joke there is. Eros (like death, figure-drawing, and the study of medicine) may at moments cause us to take it with total seriousness. The error consists in concluding that Eros should always do so and permanently abolish the joke. But this is not what happens. The very faces of all the happy lovers we know make it clear. Lovers, unless their love is very short-lived, again and again feel an element not only of comedy, not only of play, but even of buffoonery, in the body's expression of Eros. And the body would frustrate us if this were not so. It would be too clumsy an instrument to render love's music unless its very clumsiness could be felt as adding to the total experience its own grotesque charm—a sub-plot or antimasque miming with its own hearty rough-and-tumble what the soul enacts in statelier fashion. (Thus in old comedies the lyric loves of the hero and heroine are at once parodied and corroborated by some much more earthy affair between a Touchstone and an Audrey or a valet and a chambermaid.) The highest does not stand without the lowest. There is indeed at certain moments a high poetry in the flesh itself; but also, by your leave, an irreducible element of obstinate and ludicrous unpoetry. If it does not make itself felt on one occasion, it will on another. Far better plant it foursquare within the drama of Eros as comic relief than pretend you haven't noticed it.

For indeed we require this relief. The poetry is there as well as the un-poetry; the gravity of Venus as well as her levity, the *gravis ardor* or burning weight of desire. Pleasure, pushed to its extreme, shatters us like pain. The longing for a union which only the flesh can mediate while the flesh, our mutually excluding bodies, renders it forever unattainable can have the grandeur of a metaphysical pursuit. Amorousness as well as grief can bring tears to the eyes. But Venus does not always come thus "entire, fastened to her prey," and the fact that she sometimes does so is the very reason for preserving always a hint of playfulness in our attitude to her. When natural things look most divine, the demoniac is just round the corner.

This refusal to be quite immersed—this recollection of the levity even when, for the moment, only the gravity is displayed—is especially relevant to a certain attitude which Venus, in her intensity, evokes from most (I believe, not all) pairs of lovers. This act can invite the man to an extreme, though short-lived, masterfulness, to the dominance of a conqueror or a captor, and the woman to a correspondingly extreme subjection and surrender. Hence the roughness, even fierceness, of some erotic play; the "lover's pinch which hurts and is desired." How should a sane couple think of this? or a Christian couple permit it?

I think it is harmless and wholesome on one condition. We must recognise that we have here to do with what I called "the Pagan sacrament" in sex. In Friendship, as we noticed, each participant stands for precisely himself—the contingent individual he is. But in the act of love we are not merely ourselves. We are also representatives. It is here no impoverishment but an enrichment to be aware that forces older and less personal than we work through us. In us all the masculinity and femininity of the world, all that is assailant and responsive, are momentarily focused. The man does play the Sky-Father and the woman the Earth-Mother; he does play Form, and she Matter. But we must give full value to the word *play*. Of course neither "plays a part" in the sense of being a hypocrite. But each plays a part or role in—well, in something which is comparable to a mystery-play or ritual (at one extreme) and to a masque or even a charade (at the other).

A woman who accepted as literally her own this extreme self-surrender would be an idolatress offering to a man what belongs only to God. And a man would have to be the coxcomb of all coxcombs, and indeed a blasphemer, if he arrogated to himself, as the mere person he is, the sort of sovereignty to which Venus for a moment exalts him. But what cannot lawfully be yielded or claimed can be lawfully enacted. Outside this ritual or drama he and she are two immortal souls, two free-born adults, two citizens. We should be much mistaken if we supposed that those marriages where this mastery is most asserted and acknowledged in the act of Venus were those where the husband is most likely to be dominant in the married life as a whole; the reverse is perhaps more probable. But within the rite or drama they become a god and goddess between whom there is no equality—whose relations are asymmetrical.

Some will think it strange I should find an element of ritual or masquerade in that action which is often regarded as the most real, the most unmasked and sheerly genuine, we ever do. Are we not our true selves when naked? In a sense, no. The word *naked* was originally a past participle; the naked man was the man who had undergone a process of *naking*, that is, of stripping or peeling (you used the verb of nuts and fruit). Time out of mind the naked man has seemed to our ancestors not the natural but the abnormal man; not the man who has abstained from dressing but the man who has been for some reason undressed. And it is a simple fact—anyone can observe it at a men's bathing place—that nudity emphasises common humanity and soft-pedals what is individual. In that way we are "more ourselves" when clothed. By nudity the lovers cease to be solely John and Mary; the universal He and She are emphasised. You could almost say they *put* on nakedness as a ceremonial robe—or as the costume for a charade. For we must still be aware—and never more than when we thus partake of the Pagan sacrament in our love-passages—of being serious in the wrong way. The Sky-Father himself is only a Pagan dream of One far greater than Zeus and far more masculine than the male. And a mortal man is not even the Sky-Father, and cannot really wear his crown. Only a copy of it, done in tinselled paper. I do not call it this in contempt. I like ritual; I like private theatricals; I even like charades. Paper crowns have their legitimate, and (in the proper context) their serious, uses. They are not in the last resort much flimsier ("if imagination mend them") then all earthly dignities.

But I dare not mention this Pagan sacrament without turning aside to guard against any danger of confusing it with an incomparably higher mystery. As nature crowns man in that brief action, so the Christian law has crowned him in the permanent relationship of marriage, bestowing—or should I say, inflicting?—a certain "headship" on him. This is a very different coronation. And as we could easily take the natural mystery too seriously, so we might take the Christian mystery not seriously enough. Christian writers (notably Milton) have sometimes spoken of the husband's headship with a complacency to make the blood run cold. We must go back to our Bibles. The husband is the head of the wife just in so far as he is to her what Christ is to the Church. He is to love her as Christ loved the Church—read on—*and give his life for her* (*Eph.* V, 25). This headship, then, is most fully embodied not in the husband we should all wish to be but in him whose marriage is most like a crucifixion; whose wife receives most and gives least, is most unworthy of him, is—in her own mere nature—least lovable. For the Church has no beauty but what the Bride-groom gives her; he does not find, but makes her, lovely. The chrism of this terrible coronation is to be seen not in the joys of any man's marriage but in its sorrows, in the sickness and sufferings of a good wife or the faults of a bad one, in his unwearying (never paraded) care or his inexhaustible forgiveness: forgiveness, not acquiescence. As Christ sees in the flawed, proud, fanatical or lukewarm Church on earth that Bride who will one day be without spot or wrinkle, and labours to produce the latter, so the husband whose headship is Christ-like (and he is allowed no other sort) never despairs. He is a King Cophetua who after twenty years still hopes that the beggar-girl will one day learn to speak the truth and wash behind her ears.

To say this is not to say that there is any virtue or wisdom in making a marriage that involves such misery. There is no wisdom or virtue in seeking unnecessary martyrdom or deliberately courting persecution; yet it is, none the less, the persecuted or martyred Christian in whom the pattern of the Master is most unambiguously realised. So, in these terrible marriages, once they have come about, the "headship" of the husband, if only he can sustain it, is most Christ-like.

The sternest feminist need not grudge my sex the crown offered to it either in the Pagan or in the Christian mystery. For the one is of paper and the other of thorns. The real danger is not that husbands may grasp the latter too eagerly; but that they will allow or compel their wives to usurp it.

From Venus, the carnal ingredient within Eros, I now turn to Eros as a whole. Here we shall see the same pattern repeated. As Venus within Eros does not really aim at pleasure, so Eros does not aim at happiness. We may think he does, but when he is brought to the test it proves otherwise. Everyone knows that it is useless to try to separate lovers by proving to them that their marriage will be an unhappy one. This is not only because they will disbelieve you. They usually will, no doubt. But even if they believed, they would not be dissuaded.

For it is the very mark of Eros that when he is in us we had rather share unhappiness with the Beloved than be happy on any other terms. Even if the two lovers are mature and experienced people who know that broken hearts heal in the end and can clearly foresee that, if they once steeled themselves to go through the present agony of parting, they would almost certainly be happier ten years hence than marriage is at all likely to make them—even then, they would not part. To Eros all these calculations are irrelevant—just as the coolly brutal judgment of Lucretius is irrelevant to Venus. Even when it becomes clear beyond all evasion that marriage with the Beloved cannot possibly lead to happiness—when it cannot even profess to offer any other life than that of tending an incurable invalid, of hopeless poverty, of exile, or of disgrace—Eros never hesitates to say, "Better this than parting. Better to be miserable with her than happy without her. Let our hearts break provided they break together." If the voice within us does not say this, it is not the voice of Eros.

This is the grandeur and terror of love. But notice, as before, side by side with this grandeur, the playfulness. Eros, as well as Venus, is the subject of countless jokes. And even when the circumstances of the two lovers are so tragic that no bystander could keep back his tears, they themselves—in want, in hospital wards, on visitors' days in jail—will sometimes be surprised by a merriment which strikes the onlooker (but not them) as unbearably pathetic. Nothing is falser than the idea that mockery is necessarily hostile. Until they have a baby to laugh at, lovers are always laughing at each other.

It is in the grandeur of Eros that the seeds of danger are concealed. He has spoken like a god. His total commitment, his reckless disregard of happiness, his transcendence of self-regard, sound like a message from the eternal world.

And yet it cannot, just as it stands, be the voice of God Himself. For Eros, speaking with that very grandeur and displaying that very transcendence of self, may urge to evil as well as to good. Nothing is shallower than the belief that a love which leads to sin is always qualitatively lower—more animal or more trivial—than one which leads to faithful, fruitful and Christian marriage. The love which leads to cruel and perjured unions, even to suicide-pacts and murder, is not likely to be wandering lust or idle sentiment. It may well be Eros in all his splendour; heart-breakingly sincere; ready for every sacrifice except renunciation.

There have been schools of thought which accepted the voice of Eros as something actually transcendent and tried to justify the absoluteness of his commands. Plato will have it that "falling in love" is the mutual recognition on earth of souls which have been singled out for one another in a previous and celestial existence. To meet the Beloved is to realise "We loved before we were born." As a myth to express what lovers feel this is admirable. But if one accepted it literally one would be faced by an embarrassing consequence. We should have to conclude that in that heavenly and forgotten life affairs were no better managed than here. For Eros may unite the most unsuitable yokefellows; many unhappy, and predictably unhappy, marriages were love-matches.

A theory more likely to be accepted in our own day is what we may call Shavian—Shaw himself might have said "metabiological"—Romanticism. According to Shavian Romanticism the voice of Eros is the voice of

the *élan vital* or Life Force, the "evolutionary appetite."
In overwhelming a particular couple it is seeking parents
(or ancestors) for the superman. It is indifferent both to
their personal happiness and to the rules of morality
because it aims at something which Shaw thinks very
much more important: the future perfection of our species. But if all this were true it hardly makes clear
whether—and if so, why—we should obey it. All pictures yet offered us of the superman are so unattractive
that one might well vow celibacy at once to avoid the
risk of begetting him. And secondly, this theory surely
leads to the conclusion that the Life Force does not very
well understand its (or her? or his?) own business. So
far as we can see the existence or intensity of Eros between two people is no warrant that their offspring will
be especially satisfactory, or even that they will have
offspring at all. Two good "strains" (in the stockbreed-
ers' sense), not two good lovers, is the recipe for fine
children. And what on earth was the Life Force doing
through all those countless generations when the begetting of children depended very little on mutual Eros and
very much on arranged marriages, slavery, and rape? Has
it only just thought of this bright idea for improving the
species?

Neither the Platonic nor the Shavian type of erotic
transcendentalism can help a Christian. We are not wor-
shippers of the Life Force and we know nothing of previous existences. We must not give unconditional
obedience to the voice of Eros when he speaks most like
a god. Neither must we ignore or attempt to deny the
god-like quality. This love is really and truly like Love
Himself. In it there is a real nearness to God (by Resemblance); but not, therefore and necessarily, a near-

ness of Approach. Eros, honoured so far as love of God and charity to our fellows will allow, may become for us a means of Approach. His total commitment is a paradigm or example, built into our natures, of the love we ought to exercise towards God and Man. As nature, for the nature-lover, gives a content to the word *glory*, so this gives a content to the word *Charity*. It is as if Christ said to us through Eros, "Thus—just like this— with this prodigality—not counting the cost—you are to love me and the least of my brethren." Our conditional honour to Eros will of course vary with our circumstances. Of some a total renunciation (but not a contempt) is required. Others, with Eros as their fuel and also as their model, can embark on the married life. Within which Eros, of himself, will never be enough— will indeed survive only in so far as he is continually chastened and corroborated by higher principles.

But Eros, honoured without reservation and obeyed unconditionally, becomes a demon. And this is just how he claims to be honoured and obeyed. Divinely indifferent to our selfishness, he is also demoniacally rebellious to every claim of God or Man that would oppose him. Hence as the poet says:

> *People in love cannot be moved by kindness,*
> *And opposition makes them feel like martyrs.*

Martyrs is exactly right. Years ago when I wrote about medieval love-poetry and described its strange, half make-believe, "religion of love," I was blind enough to treat this as an almost purely literary phenomenon. I know better now. Eros by his nature invites it. Of all loves he is, at his height, most god-like; therefore most prone to demand our worship. Of himself he always tends to turn "being in love" into a sort of religion.

Theologians have often feared, in this love, a danger of idolatry. I think they meant by this that the lovers might idolise one another. That does not seem to me to be the real danger; certainly not in marriage. The deliciously plain prose and businesslike intimacy of married life render it absurd. So does the Affection in which Eros is almost invariably clothed. Even in courtship I question whether anyone who has felt the thirst for the Uncreated, or even dreamed of feeling it, ever supposed that the Beloved could satisfy it. As a fellow-pilgrim pierced with the very same desire, that is, as a Friend, the Beloved may be gloriously and helpfully relevant; but as an object for it—well (I would not be rude), ridiculous. The real danger seems to me not that the lovers will idolise each other but that they will idolise Eros himself.

I do not of course mean that they will build altars or say prayers to him. The idolatry I speak of can be seen in the popular misinterpretation of Our Lord's words "Her sins, which are many, are forgiven her, for she loved much" (*Luke* VII, 47). From the context, and especially from the preceding parable of the debtors, it is clear that this must mean: "The greatness of her love for Me is evidence of the greatness of the sins I have forgiven her." (The *for* here is like the *for* in "He can't have gone out, *for* his hat is still hanging in the hall"; the presence of the hat is not the cause of his being in the house but a probable proof that he is). But thousands of people take it quite differently. They first assume, with no evidence, that her sins were sins against chastity, though, for all we know, they may have been usury, dishonest shopkeeping, or cruelty to children. And they then take Our Lord to be saying, "I forgive her un-chastity because she was so much in love." The im-plication is that a great Eros extenuates—almost sanctions—almost sanctifies—any actions it leads to.

When lovers say of some act that we might blame, "Love made us do it," notice the tone. A man saying, "I did it because I was frightened," or "I did it because I was angry," speaks quite differently. He is putting forward an excuse for what he feels to require excusing. But the lovers are seldom doing quite that. Notice how tremulously, almost how devoutly, they say the word *love*, not so much pleading an "extenuating circum-stance" as appealing to an authority. The confession can be almost a boast. There can be a shade of defiance in it. They "feel like martyrs." In extreme cases what their words really express is a demure yet unshakable alle-giance to the god of love.

"These reasons in love's law have passed for good," says Milton's Dalila. That is the point; *in love's law*. "In love," we have our own "law," a religion of our own, our own god. Where a true Eros is present resistance to his commands feels like apostasy, and what are really (by the Christian standard) temptations speak with the voice of duties—quasi-religious duties, acts of pious zeal to love. He builds his own religion round the lovers. Benjamin Constant has noticed how he creates for them, in a few weeks or months, a joint past which seems to them immemorial. They recur to it continually with wonder and reverence, as the Psalmists recur to the his-tory of Israel. It is in fact the Old Testament of Love's religion; the record of love's judgments and mercies to-wards his chosen pair up to the moment when they first knew they were lovers. After that, its New Testament begins. They are now under a new law, under what corresponds (in this religion) to Grace. They are new creatures. The "spirit" of Eros supersedes all laws, and they must not "grieve" it.

It seems to sanction all sorts of actions they would not otherwise have dared. I do not mean solely, or chiefly, acts that violate chastity. They are just as likely to be acts of injustice or uncharity against the outer world. They will seem like proofs of piety and zeal towards Eros. The pair can say to one another in an almost sacrificial spirit, "It is for love's sake that I have neglected my parents—left my children—cheated my partner—failed my friend at his greatest need." These reasons in love's law have passed for good. The votaries may even come to feel a particular merit in such sacrifices; what costlier offering can be laid on love's altar than one's conscience?

And all the time the grim joke is that this Eros whose voice seems to speak from the eternal realm is not himself necessarily even permanent. He is notoriously the most mortal of our loves. The world rings with complaints of his fickleness. What is baffling is the combination of this fickleness with his protestations of permanency. To be in love is both to intend and to promise lifelong fidelity. Love makes vows unasked; can't be deterred from making them. "I will be ever true," are almost the first words he utters. Not hypocritically but sincerely. No experience will cure him of the delusion. We have all heard of people who are in love again every few years; each time sincerely convinced that "*this* time it's the real thing," that their wanderings are over, that they have found their true love and will themselves be true till death.

And yet Eros is in a sense right to make this promise.

The event of falling in love is of such a nature that we are right to reject as intolerable the idea that it should be transitory. In one high bound it has overleaped the massive wall of our selfhood; it has made appetite itself altruistic, tossed personal happiness aside as a triviality and planted the interests of another in the centre of our being. Spontaneously and without effort we have fulfilled the law (towards one person) by loving our neighbour as ourselves. It is an image, a foretaste, of what we must become to all if Love Himself rules in us without a rival. It is even (well used) a preparation for that. Simply to relapse from it, merely to "fall out of" love again, is—if I may coin the ugly word—a sort of *dis-redemption*. Eros is driven to promise what Eros of himself cannot perform.

Can we be in this selfless liberation for a lifetime? Hardly for a week. Between the best possible lovers this high condition is intermittent. The old self soon turns out to be not so dead as he pretended—as after a religious conversion. In either he may be momentarily knocked flat; he will soon be up again; if not on his feet, at least on his elbow, if not roaring, at least back to his surly grumbling or his mendicant whine. And Venus will often slip back into mere sexuality.

But these lapses will not destroy a marriage between two "decent and sensible" people. The couple whose marriage will certainly be endangered by them, and possibly ruined, are those who have idolised Eros. They thought he had the power and truthfulness of a god. They expected that mere feeling would do for them, and permanently, all that was necessary. When this expectation is disappointed they throw the blame on Eros or, more usually, on their partners. In reality, however,

EROS

Eros, having made his gigantic promise and shown you in glimpses what its performance would be like, has "done his stuff." He, like a godparent, makes the vows; it is we who must keep them. It is we who must labour to bring our daily life into even closer accordance with what the glimpses have revealed. We must do the works of Eros when Eros is not present. This all good lovers know, though those who are not reflective or articulate will be able to express it only in a few conventional phrases about "taking the rough along with the smooth," not "expecting too much," having "a little common sense," and the like. And all good Christian lovers know that this programme, modest as it sounds, will not be carried out except by humility, charity and divine grace; that it is indeed the whole Christian life seen from one particular angle.

Thus Eros, like the other loves, but more strikingly because of his strength, sweetness, terror and high port, reveals his true status. He cannot of himself be what, nevertheless, he must be if he is to remain Eros. He needs help; therefore needs to be ruled. The god dies or becomes a demon unless he obeys God. It would be well if, in such case, he always died. But he may live on, mercilessly chaining together two mutual tormentors, each raw all over with the poison of hate-in-love, each ravenous to receive and implacably refusing to give, jealous, suspicious, resentful, struggling for the upper hand, determined to be free and to allow no freedom, living on "scenes." Read *Anna Karenina*, and do not fancy that such things happen only in Russia. The lovers' old hyperbole of "eating" each other can come horribly near to the truth.

CHARITY

William Morris wrote a poem called "Love Is Enough" and someone is said to have reviewed it briefly in the words "It isn't." Such has been the burden of this book. The natural loves are not self-sufficient. Something else, at first vaguely described as "decency and common sense," but later revealed as goodness, and finally as the whole Christian life in one particular relation, must come to the help of the mere feeling if the feeling is to be kept sweet.

To say this is not to belittle the natural loves but to indicate where their real glory lies. It is no disparagement to a garden to say that it will not fence and weed itself, nor prune its own fruit trees, nor roll and cut its own lawns. A garden is a good thing but that is not the sort of goodness it has. It will remain a garden, as distinct from a wilderness, only if someone does all these things to it. Its real glory is of quite a different kind. The very fact that it needs constant weeding and pruning bears witness to that glory. It teems with life. It glows with colour and smells like heaven and puts forward at every hour of a summer day beauties which man could never have created and could not even, on his own resources, have imagined. If you want to see the difference between its contribution and the gardener's, put the commonest weed it grows side by side with his hoes, rakes, shears, and packet of weed killer; you have put beauty, energy and fecundity beside dead, sterile things. Just so, our "decency and common sense" show grey and deathlike beside the geniality of love. And when the garden is in its full glory the gardener's contributions to that glory will still have been in a sense paltry compared with those of nature. Without life springing from the earth, without rain, light and heat descending from the sky, he could do nothing. When he has done all, he has merely encouraged here and discouraged there, powers and beauties that have a different source. But his share, though small, is indispensable and laborious. When God planted a garden He set a man over it and set the man under Himself. When He planted the garden of our nature and caused the flowering, fruiting loves to grow there, He set our will to "dress" them. Compared with them it is dry and cold. And unless His grace comes down, like the rain and the sunshine, we shall use this tool to little purpose. But its laborious—and largely negative—services are indispensable. If they were needed when the garden was still Paradisal, how much more now when the soil has gone sour and the worst weeds seem to thrive on it best? But heaven forbid we should work in the spirit of prigs and Stoics. While we hack and prune we know very well that what we are hacking and pruning is big with a splendour and vitality which our rational will could never of itself have supplied. To liberate that splendour, to let it become fully what it is trying to be, to have tall trees instead of scrubby tangles, and sweet apples instead of crabs, is part of our purpose.

But only part. For now we must face a topic that I have long postponed. Hitherto hardly anything has been said in this book about our natural loves as rivals to the love of God. Now the question can no longer be avoided. There were two reasons for my delay.

One—already hinted—is that this question is not the place at which most of us need begin. It is seldom, at the outset, "addressed to our condition." For most of us the true rivalry lies between the self and the human Other, not yet between the human Other and God. It is dangerous to press upon a man the duty of getting beyond earthly love when his real difficulty lies in getting so far. And it is no doubt easy enough to love the fellow-creature less and to imagine that this is happening because we are learning to love God more, when the real reason may be quite different. We may be only "mistaking the decays of nature for the increase of Grace." Many people do not find it really difficult to hate their wives or mothers. M. Mauriac, in a fine scene, pictures the other disciples stunned and bewildered by this strange command, but not Judas. He laps it up easily.

But to have stressed the rivalry earlier in this book would have been premature in another way also. The claim to divinity which our loves so easily make can be refuted without going so far as that. The loves prove that they are unworthy to take the place of God by the fact that they cannot even remain themselves and do what they promise to do without God's help. Why prove that some petty princeling is not the lawful Emperor when without the Emperor's support he cannot even keep his subordinate throne and make peace in his little province for half a year? Even for their own sakes the loves must submit to be second things if they are to remain the things they want to be. In this yoke lies their true freedom; they "are taller when they bow." For when God rules in a human heart, though He may sometimes have to remove certain of its native authorities altogether, He often continues others in their offices and, by subjecting their authority to His, gives it for the first time a firm basis. Emerson has said, "When half-gods go, the gods arrive." That is a very doubtful maxim. Better say, "When God arrives (and only then) the half-gods can remain." Left to themselves they either vanish or become demons. Only in His name can they with beauty and security "wield their little tridents." The rebellious slogan "All for love" is really love's death warrant (date of execution, for the moment, left blank).

But the question of the rivalry, for these reasons long postponed, must now be treated. In any earlier period, except the nineteenth century, it would have loomed large throughout a book on this subject. If the Victorians needed the reminder that love is not enough, older theologians were always saying very loudly that (natural) love is likely to be a great deal too much. The danger of loving our fellow-creatures too little was less present to their minds than that of loving them idolatrously. In every wife, mother, child and friend they saw a possible rival to God. So of course does Our Lord (*Luke* XIV, 26).

There is one method of dissuading us from inordinate

love of the fellow-creature which I find myself forced to reject at the very outset. I do so with trembling, for it met me in the pages of a great saint and a great thinker to whom my own glad debts are incalculable.

In words which can still bring tears to the eyes, St. Augustine describes the desolation into which the death of his friend Nebridius plunged him (*Confessions* IV, 10). Then he draws a moral. This is what comes, he says, of giving one's heart to anything but God. All human beings pass away. Do not let your happiness depend on something you may lose. If love is to be a blessing, not a misery, it must be for the only Beloved who will never pass away.

Of course this is excellent sense. Don't put your goods in a leaky vessel. Don't spend too much on a house you may be turned out of. And there is no man alive who responds more naturally than I to such canny maxims. I am a safety-first creature. Of all arguments against love none makes so strong an appeal to my nature as "Careful! This might lead you to suffering."

To my nature, my temperament, yes. Not to my conscience. When I respond to that appeal I seem to myself to be a thousand miles away from Christ. If I am sure of anything I am sure that His teaching was never meant to confirm my congenital preference for safe investments and limited liabilities. I doubt whether there is anything in me that pleases Him less. And who could conceivably begin to love God on such a prudential ground—because the security (so to speak) is better? Who could even include it among the grounds for loving? Would you choose a wife or a Friend—if it comes to that, would you choose a dog—in this spirit? One must be outside the world of love, of all loves, before one thus calculates.

Eros, lawless Eros, preferring the Beloved to happiness, is more like Love himself than this.

I think that this passage in the *Confessions* is less a part of St. Augustine's Christendom than a hangover from the high-minded Pagan philosophies in which he grew up. It is closer to Stoic "apathy" or neo-Platonic mysticism than to charity. We follow One who wept over Jerusalem and at the grave of Lazarus, and, loving all, yet had one disciple whom, in a special sense, he "loved." St. Paul has a higher authority with us than St. Augustine—St. Paul who shows no sign that he would not have suffered like a man, and no feeling that he ought not so to have suffered, if Epaphroditus had died (*Phil.* II, 27).

Even if it were granted that insurances against heartbreak were our highest wisdom, does God Himself offer them? Apparently not. Christ comes at last to say "Why hast thou forsaken me?"

There is no escape along the lines St. Augustine suggests. Nor along any other lines. There is no safe investment. To love at all is to be vulnerable. Love anything, and your heart will certainly be wrung and possibly be broken. If you want to make sure of keeping it intact, you must give your heart to no one, not even to an animal. Wrap it carefully round with hobbies and little luxuries; avoid all entanglements; lock it up safe in the casket or coffin of your selfishness. But in that casket—safe, dark, motionless, airless—it will change. It will not be broken; it will become unbreakable, impenetrable, irredeemable. The alternative to tragedy, or at least to the risk of tragedy, is damnation. The only place outside Heaven where you can be perfectly safe from all the dangers and perturbations of love is Hell.

I believe that the most lawless and inordinate loves are less contrary to God's will than a self-invited and self-protective lovelessness. It is like hiding the talent in a napkin and for much the same reason "I knew thee that thou wert a hard man." Christ did not teach and suffer that we might become, even in the natural loves, more careful of our own happiness. If a man is not uncalculating towards the earthly beloveds whom he has seen, he is none the more likely to be so towards God whom he has not. We shall draw nearer to God, not by trying to avoid the sufferings inherent in all loves, but by accepting them and offering them to Him; throwing away all defensive armour. If our hearts need to be broken, and if He chooses this as the way in which they should break, so be it.

It remains certainly true that all natural loves can be inordinate. *Inordinate* does not mean "insufficiently cautious." Nor does it mean "too big." It is not a quantitative term. It is probably impossible to love any human being simply "too much." We may love him too much *in proportion* to our love for God; but it is the smallness of our love for God, not the greatness of our love for the man, that constitutes the inordinacy. But even this must be refined upon. Otherwise we shall trouble some who are very much on the right road but alarmed because they cannot feel towards God so warm a sensible emotion as they feel for the earthly Beloved. It is much to be wished—at least I think so—that we all, at all times, could. We must pray that this gift should be given us. But the question whether we are loving God or the earthly Beloved "more" is not, so far as concerns our Christian duty, a question about the comparative intensity of two feelings. The real question is, which (when the alternative comes) do you serve, or choose, or put first? To which claim does your will, in the last resort, yield?

As so often, Our Lord's own words are both far fiercer and far more tolerable than those of the theologians. He says nothing about guarding against earthly loves for fear we might be hurt; He says something that cracks like a whip about trampling them all under foot the moment they hold us back from following Him. "If any man come to me and hate not his father and mother and wife . . . and his own life also, he cannot be my disciple" (*Luke* XIV, 26).

But how are we to understand the word *hate*? That Love Himself should be commanding what we ordinarily mean by hatred—commanding us to cherish resentment, to gloat over another's misery, to delight in injuring him—is almost a contradiction in terms. I think Our Lord, in the sense here intended, "hated" St. Peter when he said, "Get thee behind me." To hate is to reject, to set one's face against, to make no concession to, the Beloved when the Beloved utters, however sweetly and however pitiably, the suggestions of the Devil. A man, said Jesus, who tries to serve two masters, will "hate" the one and "love" the other. It is not, surely, mere feelings of aversion and liking that are here in question. He will adhere to, consent to, work for, the one and not for the other. Consider again, "I loved Jacob and I *hated* Esau" (*Malachi* I, 2–3). How is the thing called God's "hatred" of Esau displayed in the actual story? Not at all as we might expect. There is of course no ground for assuming that Esau made a bad end and was a lost soul; the Old Testament, here as elsewhere, has nothing to say about such matters. And, from all we are told, Esau's earthly life was, in every ordinary sense, a good deal more blessed than Jacob's. It is Jacob who has all the disappointments, humiliations, terrors, and bereavements. But he has something which Esau has not. He is a patriarch. He hands on the Hebraic tradition, transmits the vocation and the blessing, becomes an ancestor of Our Lord. The "loving" of Jacob seems to mean the acceptance of Jacob for a high (and painful) vocation; the "hating" of Esau, his rejection. He is "turned down," fails to "make the grade," is found useless for the purpose. So, in the last resort, we must turn down or disqualify our nearest and dearest when they come between us and our obedience to God. Heaven knows, it will seem to them sufficiently like hatred. We must not act on the pity we feel; we must be blind to tears and deaf to pleadings.

I will not say that this duty is hard; some find it too easy; some, hard almost beyond endurance. What is hard for all is to know when the occasion for such "hating" has arisen. Our temperaments deceive us. The meek and tender—uxorious husbands, submissive wives, doting parents, dutiful children—will not easily believe that it has ever arrived. Self-assertive people, with a dash of the bully in them, will believe it too soon. That is why it is of such extreme importance so to order our loves that it is unlikely to arrive at all.

How this could come about we may see on a far lower level when the Cavalier poet, going to the wars, says to his mistress:

> *I could not love thee, dear, so much*
> *Loved I not honour more.*

There are women to whom the plea would be meaning-less. *Honour* would be just one of those silly things that Men talk about; a verbal excuse for, therefore an aggra-vation of, the offence against "love's law" which the poet is about to commit. Lovelace can use it with con-fidence because his lady is a Cavalier lady who already admits, as he does, the claims of Honour. He does not need to "hate" her, to set his face against her, for he and she acknowledge the same law. They have agreed and understood each other on this matter long before. The task of converting her to a belief in Honour is not now—now, when the decision is upon them—to be un-dertaken. It is this prior agreement which is so necessary when a far greater claim than that of Honour is at stake. It is too late, when the crisis comes, to begin telling a wife or husband or mother or friend, that your love all along had a secret reservation—"under God" or "so far as a higher Love permits." They ought to have been warned; not, to be sure, explicitly, but by the implication of a thousand talks, by the principle revealed in a hundred decisions upon small matters. Indeed, a real disagreement on this issue should make itself felt early enough to prevent a marriage or a Friendship from ex-isting at all. The best love of either sort is not blind. Oliver Elton, speaking of Carlyle and Mill, said that they differed about justice, and that such a difference was naturally fatal "to any friendship worthy of the name." If "All"—quite seriously all—"for love" is im-plicit in the Beloved's attitude, his or her love is not worth having. It is not related in the right way to Love Himself.

And this brings me to the foot of the last steep ascent

this book must try to make. We must try to relate the human activities called "loves" to that Love which is God a little more precisely than we have yet done. The precision can, of course, be only that of a model or a symbol, certain to fail us in the long run and, even while we use it, requiring correction from other models. The humblest of us, in a state of Grace, can have some "knowledge-by-acquaintance" (*connaître*), some "tasting," of Love Himself; but man even at his highest sanctity and intelligence has no direct "knowledge about" (*savoir*) the ultimate Being—only analogies. We cannot see light, though by light we can see things. Statements about God are extrapolations from the knowledge of other things which the divine illumination enables us to know. I labour these deprecations because, in what follows, my efforts to be clear (and not intolerably lengthy) may suggest a confidence which I by no means feel. I should be mad if I did. Take it as one man's reverie, almost one man's myth. If anything in it is useful to you, use it; if anything is not, never give it a second thought.

God is love. Again, "Herein is love, not that we loved God but that He loved us" (1 *John* IV, 10). We must not begin with mysticism, with the creature's love for God, or with the wonderful foretastes of the fruition of God vouchsafed to some in their earthly life. We begin at the real beginning, with love as the Divine energy. This primal love is Gift-love. In God there is no hunger that needs to be filled, only plenteousness that desires to give. The doctrine that God was under no necessity to create is not a piece of dry scholastic speculation. It is essential. Without it we can hardly avoid the conception of what I can only call a "managerial" God; a Being whose function or nature is to "run" the universe, who stands to it as a head-master to a school or a hotelier to a hotel. But to be sovereign of the universe is no great matter to God. In Himself, at home in "the land of the Trinity," he is Sovereign of a far greater realm. We must keep always before our eyes that vision of Lady Julian's in which God carried in His hand a little object like a nut, and that nut was "all that is made." God, who needs nothing, loves into existence wholly superfluous creatures in order that He may love and perfect them. He creates the universe, already foreseeing—or should we say "seeing"? there are no tenses in God—the buzzing cloud of flies about the cross, the flayed back pressed against the uneven stake, the nails driven through the mesial nerves, the repeated incipient suffocation as the body droops, the repeated torture of back and arms as it is time after time, for breath's sake, hitched up. If I may dare the biological image, God is a "host" who deliberately creates His own parasites; causes us to be that we may exploit and "take advantage of" Him. Herein is love. This is the diagram of Love Himself, the inventor of all loves.

God, as Creator of nature, implants in us both Gift-loves and Need-loves. The Gift-loves are natural images of Himself; proximities to Him by resemblance which are not necessarily and in all men proximities of approach. A devoted mother, a beneficent ruler or teacher, may give and give, continually exhibiting the likeness, without making the approach. The Need-loves, so far as I have been able to see, have no resemblance to the Love which God is. They are rather correlatives, opposites; not as evil is the opposite of good, of course, but as the form of the blanc-mange is an opposite to the form of the mould.

But in addition to these natural loves God can bestow a far better gift; or rather, since our minds must divide and pigeon-hole, two gifts.

He communicates to men a share of His own Gift-love. This is different from the Gift-loves He has built into their nature. These never quite seek simply the good of the loved object for the object's own sake. They are biased in favour of those goods they can themselves be-stow, or those which they would like best themselves, or those which fit in with a pre-conceived picture of the life they want the object to lead. But Divine Gift-love— Love Himself working in a man—is wholly disinter-ested and desires what is simply best for the beloved. Again, natural Gift-love is always directed to objects which the lover finds in some way intrinsically lovable— objects to which Affection or Eros or a shared point of view attracts him, or, failing that, to the grateful and the deserving, or perhaps to those whose helplessness is of a winning and appealing kind. But Divine Gift-love in the man enables him to love what is not naturally lovable; lepers, criminals, enemies, morons, the sulky, the superior and the sneering. Finally, by a high paradox, God enables men to have a Gift-love towards Himself. There is of course a sense in which no one can give to God anything which is not already His; and if it is al-ready His what have you given? But since it is only too obvious that we can withhold ourselves, our wills and hearts, from God, we can, in that sense, also give them. What is His by right and would not exist for a moment if it ceased to be His (as the song is the singer's), He has nevertheless made ours in such a way that we can freely offer it back to Him. "Our wills are ours to make them Thine." And as all Christians know there is another way of giving to God; every stranger whom we feed or clothe is Christ. And this apparently is Gift-love to God whether we know it or not. Love Himself can work in those who know nothing of Him. The "sheep" in the parable had no idea either of the God hidden in the prisoner whom they visited or of the God hidden in themselves when they made the visit. (I take the whole parable to be about the judgment of the heathen. For it begins by saying, in the Greek, that the Lord will summon all "the nations" before Him—presumably, the Gentiles, the *Goyim*.)

That such a Gift-love comes by Grace and should be called Charity, everyone will agree. But I have to add something which will not perhaps be so easily admitted. God, as it seems to me, bestows two other gifts; a supernatural Need-love of Himself and a supernatural Need-love of one another. By the first I do not mean the Appreciative love of Himself, the gift of adoration. What little I have to say on that higher—that highest—subject will come later. I mean a love which does not dream of disinterestedness, a bottomless indigence. Like a river making its own channel, like a magic wine which in being poured out should simultaneously create the glass that was to hold it, God turns our need of Him into Need-love of Him. What is stranger still is that He creates in us a more than natural receptivity of Charity from our fellow-men. Need is so near greed and we are so greedy already that it seems a strange grace. But I cannot get it out of my head that this is what happens.

Let us consider first this supernatural Need-love of

Himself, bestowed by Grace. Of course the Grace does not create the need. That is there already; "given" (as the mathematicians say) in the mere fact of our being creatures, and incalculably increased by our being fallen creatures. What the Grace gives is the full recognition, the sensible awareness, the complete acceptance—even, with certain reservations, the glad acceptance—of this Need. For, without Grace, our wishes and our necessities are in conflict.

All those expressions of unworthiness which Christian practice puts into the believer's mouth seem to the outer world like the degraded and insincere grovellings of a sycophant before a tyrant, or at best a *façon de parler* like the self-depreciation of a Chinese gentleman when he calls himself "this coarse and illiterate person." In reality, however, they express the continually renewed, because continually necessary, attempt to negate that misconception of ourselves and of our relation to God which nature, even while we pray, is always recommending to us. No sooner do we believe that God loves us than there is an impulse to believe that He does so, not because He is Love, but because we are intrinsically lovable. The Pagans obeyed this impulse unabashed; a good man was "dear to the gods" because he was good. We, being better taught, resort to subterfuge. Far be it from us to think that we have virtues for which God could love us. But then, how magnificently we have repented! As Bunyan says, describing his first and illusory conversion, "I thought there was no man in England that pleased God better than I." Beaten out of this, we next offer our own humility to God's admiration. Surely He'll like *that*? Or if not that, our clear-sighted and humble recognition that we still lack humility. Thus, depth beneath depth and subtlety within subtlety, there remains some lingering idea of our own, our very own, attractiveness. It is easy to acknowledge, but almost impossible to realise for long, that we are mirrors whose brightness, if we are bright, is wholly derived from the sun that shines upon us. Surely we must have a little—however little—native luminosity? Surely we can't be *quite* creatures?

For this tangled absurdity of a Need, even a Need-love, which never fully acknowledges its own neediness, Grace substitutes a full, childlike and delighted acceptance of our Need, a joy in total dependence. We become "jolly beggars." The good man is sorry for the sins which have increased his Need. He is not entirely sorry for the fresh Need they have produced. And he is not sorry at all for the innocent Need that is inherent in his creaturely condition. For all the time this illusion to which nature clings as her last treasure, this pretence that we have anything of our own or could for one hour retain by our own strength any goodness that God may pour into us, has kept us from being happy. We have been like bathers who want to keep their feet—or one foot—or one toe—on the bottom, when to lose that foothold would be to surrender themselves to a glorious tumble in the surf. The consequences of parting with our last claim to intrinsic freedom, power, or worth, are real freedom, power and worth, really ours just because God gives them and because we know them to be (in another sense) not "ours." Anodos has got rid of his shadow.

But God also transforms our Need-love for one another, and it requires equal transformation. In reality we all need at times, some of us at most times, that Charity from others which, being Love Himself in them, loves the unlovable. But this, though a sort of love we need, is not the sort we want. We want to be loved for our cleverness, beauty, generosity, fairness, usefulness. The first hint that anyone is offering us the highest love of all is a terrible shock. This is so well recognised that spiteful people will pretend to be loving us with Charity precisely because they know that it will wound us. To say to one who expects a renewal of Affection, Friendship, or Eros, "I forgive you as a Christian" is merely a way of continuing the quarrel. Those who say it are of course lying. But the thing would not be falsely said in order to wound unless, if it were true, it would be wounding.

How difficult it is to receive, and to go on receiving, from others a love that does not depend on our own attraction can be seen from an extreme case. Suppose yourself a man struck down shortly after marriage by an incurable disease which may not kill you for many years; useless, impotent, hideous, disgusting; dependent on your wife's earnings; impoverishing where you hoped to enrich; impaired even in intellect and shaken by gusts of uncontrollable temper, full of unavoidable demands. And suppose your wife's care and pity to be inexhaustible. The man who can take this sweetly, who can receive all and give nothing without resentment, who can abstain even from those tiresome self-depreciations which are really only a demand for petting and reassurance, is doing something which Need-love in its merely natural condition could not attain. (No doubt such a wife will also be doing something beyond the reach of a natural Gift-love, but that is not the point at present.) In such a case to receive is harder and perhaps more blessed than to give. But what the extreme example illustrates is universal. We are all receiving Charity. There is something in each of us that cannot be naturally loved. It is no one's fault if they do not so love it. Only the lovable can be naturally loved. You might as well ask people to like the taste of rotten bread or the sound of a mechanical drill. We can be forgiven, and pitied, and loved in spite of it, with Charity; no other way. All who have good parents, wives, husbands, or children, may be sure that at some times—and perhaps at all times in respect of some one particular trait or habit—they are receiving Charity, are loved not because they are lovable but because Love Himself is in those who love them.

Thus God, admitted to the human heart, transforms not only Gift-love but Need-love; not only our Need-love of Him, but our Need-love of one another. This is of course not the only thing that can happen. He may come on what seems to us a more dreadful mission and demand that a natural love be totally renounced. A high and terrible vocation, like Abraham's, may constrain a man to turn his back on his own people and his father's house. Eros, directed to a forbidden object, may have to be sacrificed. In such instances, the process, though hard to endure, is easy to understand. What we are more likely to overlook is the necessity for a transformation even when the natural love is allowed to continue.

In such a case the Divine Love does not *substitute* itself for the natural—as if we had to throw away our silver to make room for the gold. The natural loves are summoned to become modes of Charity while also remaining the natural loves they were.

One sees here at once a sort of echo or rhyme or corollary to the Incarnation itself. And this need not surprise us, for the Author of both is the same. As Christ is perfect God and perfect Man, the natural loves are called to become perfect Charity and also perfect natural loves. As God becomes Man "Not by conversion of the Godhead into flesh, but by taking of the Manhood into God," so here; Charity does not dwindle into merely natural love but natural love is taken up into, made the tuned and obedient instrument of, Love Himself.

How this can happen, most Christians know. All the activities (sins only excepted) of the natural loves can in a favoured hour become works of the glad and shameless and grateful Need-love or of the selfless, unofficious Gift-love, which are both Charity. Nothing is either too trivial or too animal to be thus transformed. A game, a joke, a drink together, idle chat, a walk, the act of Venus—all these can be modes in which we forgive or accept forgiveness, in which we console or are reconciled, in which we "seek not our own." Thus in our very instincts, appetites and recreations, Love has prepared for Himself "a body."

But I said "in a favoured hour." Hours soon pass. The total and secure transformation of a natural love into a mode of Charity is a work so difficult that perhaps no fallen man has ever come within sight of doing it perfectly. Yet the law that loves must be so transformed is, I suppose, inexorable.

One difficulty is that here, as usual, we can take a wrong turn. A Christian—a somewhat too vocally Christian—circle or family, having grasped this principle, can make a show, in their overt behaviour and especially in their words, of having achieved the thing itself—an elaborate, fussy, embarrassing and intolerable show. Such people make every trifle a matter of explicitly spiritual importance—out loud and to one another (to

God, on their knees, behind a closed door, it would be another matter). They are always unnecessarily asking, or insufferably offering, forgiveness. Who would not rather live with those ordinary people who get over their tantrums (and ours) unemphatically, letting a meal, a night's sleep, or a joke mend all? The real work must be, of all our works, the most secret. Even as far as possible secret from ourselves. Our right hand must not know what our left is doing. We have not got far enough if we play a game of cards with the children "merely" to amuse them or to show that they are forgiven. If this is the best we can do we are right to do it. But it would be better if a deeper, less conscious, Charity threw us into a frame of mind in which a little fun with the children was the thing we should at that moment like best.

We are, however, much helped in this necessary work by that very feature of our experience at which we most repine. The invitation to turn our natural loves into Charity is never lacking. It is provided by those frictions and frustrations that meet us in all of them; unmistakable evidence that (natural) love is not going to be "enough"— unmistakable, unless we are blinded by egotism. When we are, we use them absurdly. "If only I had been more fortunate in my children (that boy gets more like his father every day) I could have loved them perfectly." But every child is sometimes infuriating; most children are not infrequently odious. "If only my husband were more considerate, less lazy, less extravagant" . . . "If only my wife had fewer moods and more sense, and were less extravagant" . . . "If my father wasn't so infernally prosy and close-fisted." But in everyone, and of course in ourselves, there is that which requires forbearance, tolerance, forgiveness. The necessity of practising these virtues first sets us, forces us, upon the attempt to turn—more strictly, to let God turn—our love into Charity. These frets and rubs are beneficial. It may even be that where there are fewest of them the conversion of natural love is most difficult. When they are plentiful the necessity of rising above it is obvious. To rise above it when it is as fully satisfied and as little impeded as earthly conditions allow—to see that we must rise when all seems so well already—this may require a subtler conversion and a more delicate insight. In this way also it may be hard for "the rich" to enter the Kingdom.

And yet, I believe, the necessity for the conversion is inexorable; at least, if our natural loves are to enter the heavenly life. That they can enter it most of us in fact believe. We may hope that the resurrection of the body means also the resurrection of what may be called our "greater body"; the general fabric of our earthly life with its affections and relationships. But only on a condition; not a condition arbitrarily laid down by God, but one necessarily inherent in the character of Heaven: nothing can enter there which cannot become heavenly. "Flesh and blood," mere nature, cannot inherit that Kingdom. Man can ascend to Heaven only because the Christ, who died and ascended to Heaven, is "formed in him." Must we not suppose that the same is true of a man's loves? Only those into which Love Himself has entered will ascend to Love Himself. And these can be raised with Him only if they have, in some degree and fashion, shared His death; if the natural element in them has submitted—year after year, or in some sudden agony— to transmutation. The fashion of this world passes away. The very name of nature implies the transitory. Natural loves can hope for eternity only in so far as they have allowed themselves to be taken into the eternity of Charity; have at least allowed the process to begin here on earth, before the night comes when no man can work. And the process will always involve a kind of death. There is no escape. In my love for wife or friend the only eternal element is the transforming presence of Love Himself. By that presence, if at all, the other elements may hope, as our physical bodies hope, to be raised from the dead. For this only is holy in them, this only is the Lord.

Theologians have sometimes asked whether we shall "know one another" in Heaven, and whether the particular love-relations worked out on earth would then continue to have any significance. It seems reasonable to reply: "It may depend what kind of love it had become, or was becoming, on earth." For, surely, to meet in the eternal world someone for whom your love in this, however strong, had been merely natural, would not be (on that ground) even interesting. Would it not be like meeting in adult life someone who had seemed to be a great friend at your preparatory school solely because of common interests and occupations? If there was nothing more, if he was not a kindred soul, he will now be a total stranger. Neither of you now plays conkers. You no longer want to swop your help with his French exercise for his help with your arithmetic. In Heaven I suspect, a love that had never embodied Love Himself would be equally irrelevant. For Nature has passed away. All that is not eternal is eternally out of date.

But I must not end on this note, I dare not—and all the less because longings and terrors of my own prompt me to do so—leave any bereaved and desolate reader confirmed in the widespread illusion that reunion with the loved dead is the goal of the Christian life. The denial of this may sound harsh and unreal in the ears of the broken hearted, but it must be denied.

"Thou hast made us for thyself," said St. Augustine, "and our heart has no rest till it comes to Thee." This, so easy to believe for a brief moment before the altar or, perhaps, half-praying, half-meditating in an April wood, sounds like mockery beside a deathbed. But we shall be far more truly mocked if, casting this way, we pin our comfort on the hope—perhaps even with the aid of *séance* and necromancy—of some day, this time forever, enjoying the earthly Beloved again, and no more. It is hard not to imagine that such an endless prolongation of earthly happiness would be completely satisfying.

But, if I may trust my own experience, we get at once a sharp warning that there is something wrong. The moment we attempt to use our faith in the other world for this purpose, that faith weakens. The moments in my life when it was really strong have all been moments when God Himself was central in my thoughts. Believing in Him, I could then believe in Heaven as a corollary. But the reverse process—believing first in reunion with the Beloved, and then, for the sake of that reunion, believing in Heaven, and finally, for the sake of Heaven, believing in God—this will not work. One can of course imagine things. But a self-critical person will soon be increasingly aware that the imagination at work is his own; he knows he is only weaving a fantasy. And simpler souls will find the phantoms they try to feed on void of all comfort and nourishment, only to be stimulated into some semblance of reality by pitiful efforts of self-hypnotism, and perhaps by the aid of ignoble pictures and hymns and (what is worse) witches.

We find thus by experience that there is no good applying to Heaven for earthly comfort. Heaven can give heavenly comfort; no other kind. And earth cannot give earthly comfort either. There is no earthly comfort in the long run.

For the dream of finding our end, the thing we were made for, in a Heaven of purely human love could not be true unless our whole Faith were wrong. We were made for God. Only by being in some respect like Him, only by being a manifestation of His beauty, loving-kindness, wisdom or goodness, has any earthly Beloved excited our love. It is not that we have loved them too much, but that we did not quite understand what we were loving. It is not that we shall be asked to turn from them, so dearly familiar, to a Stranger. When we see the face of God we shall know that we have always known it. He has been a party to, has made, sustained and moved moment by moment within, all our earthly experiences of innocent love. All that was true love in them was, even on earth, far more His than ours, and ours only because His. In Heaven there will be no anguish and no duty of turning away from our earthly Beloveds. First, because we shall have turned already; from the portraits to the Original, from the rivulets to the Fountain, from the creatures He made lovable to Love Himself. But secondly, because we shall find them all in Him. By loving Him more than them we shall love them more than we now do.

But all that is far away in "the land of the Trinity," not here in exile, in the weeping valley. Down here it is all loss and renunciation. The very purpose of the bereavement (so far as it affects ourselves) may have been to force this upon us. We are then compelled to try to believe, what we cannot yet feel, that God is our true Beloved. That is why bereavement is in some ways easier for the unbeliever than for us. He can storm and rage and shake his fist at the universe, and (if he is a genius) write poems like Housman's or Hardy's. But we, at our lowest ebb, when the least effort seems too much for us, must begin to attempt what seem impossibilities.

"Is it easy to love God?" asks an old author. "It is easy," he replies, "to those who do it." I have included two Graces under the word Charity. But God can give a third. He can awake in man, towards Himself, a supernatural Appreciative love. This is of all gifts the most to be desired. Here, not in our natural loves, nor even in ethics, lies the true centre of all human and angelic life. With this all things are possible.

And with this, where a better book would begin, mine must end. I dare not proceed. God knows, not I, whether I have ever tasted this love. Perhaps I have only imagined the tasting. Those like myself whose imagination far exceeds their obedience are subject to a just penalty; we easily imagine conditions far higher than any we have really reached. If we describe what we have imagined we may make others, and make ourselves, believe that we have really been there. And if I have only imagined it, is it a further delusion that even the imagining has at some moments made all other objects of desire—yes, even peace, to have no more fears—look like broken toys and faded flowers? Perhaps. Perhaps, for many of us, all experience merely defines, so to speak, the shape of that gap where our love of God ought to be. It is not enough. It is something. If we cannot "practise the presence of God," it is something to practise the absence of God, to become increasingly aware of our unawareness till we feel like men who should stand beside a great cataract and hear no noise, or like a man in a story who looks in a mirror and finds no face there, or a man in a dream who stretches out his hand to visible objects and gets no sensation of touch. To know that one is dreaming is to be no longer perfectly asleep. But for news of the fully waking world you must go to my betters.